THE GREAT LIVES SERIES

Great Lives biographies shed an exciting new light on the many dynamic men and women whose actions, visions, and dedication to an ideal have influenced the course of history. Their ambitions, dreams, successes and failures, the controversies they faced and the obstacles they overcame are the true stories behind these distinguished world leaders, explorers, and great Americans.

Other biographies in the Great Lives Series

ACKNOWLEDGMENT

A special thanks to educators Dr. Frank Moretti, Ph.D., Associate Headmaster of the Dalton School in New York City; Dr. Paul Mattingly, Ph.D., Professor of History at New York University; and Barbara Smith, M.S., Assistant Superintendent of the Los Angeles Unified School District, for their contributions to the Great Lives Series.

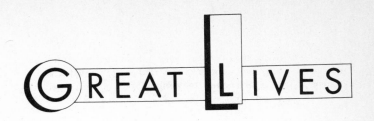

LEWIS AND CLARK
Leading America West
Steven Otfinoski

FAWCETT COLUMBINE
NEW YORK

For middle-school readers

A Fawcett Columbine Book
Published by Ballantine Books

Library of Congress Catalog Card Number: 90-92953

ISBN 0-449-90398-2

Cover design and illustration by Paul Davis Studio

Manufactured in the United States of America

First Edition: April 1992

10 9 8 7 6 5 4 3 2 1

TABLE OF CONTENTS

LEWIS AND CLARK

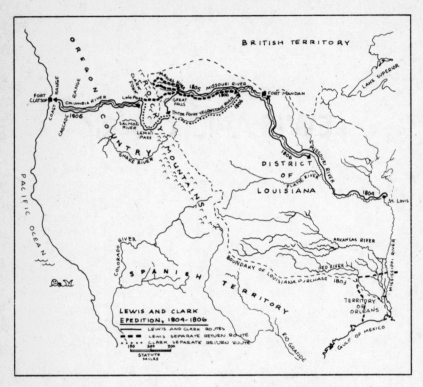

The route taken by the Corps of Discovery.

1

The Terrible Mountains

THE ROCKY SLOPES of the Bitterroot Mountain loomed ahead like an invincible giant for the weary party of thirty-odd men, one woman and a child that made up the Corps of Discovery. A year and a half earlier, at President Jefferson's request, Captain Meriwether Lewis and his partner, William Clark, set out on an expedition across the unexplored American West. Their mission? To discover an overland route to the Pacific Ocean, something which no one of European descent had ever done. They had crossed the entire midwest, and were finally crossing the Rocky Mountains. The journey had become so difficult, it looked as if the Corps of Discovery would be defeated by the miserable land.

As freezing rain pelted them mercilessly, one man lost his footing on the steep, treacherous trail and fell. Captain Lewis grabbed the man by his buckskin shirt and helped him to his feet again. A few moments later a weak colt, burdened with a heavy load, whinnied once and slipped. Even the animal's hoofed feet were no match for the icy mountain trail. Three men helped the colt to its feet again and onward they trudged through the dark, chilly afternoon.

A short time later Lewis and his partner William Clark called for the party to stop for the night and set up camp. Men and animals collapsed alike with relief. They were bone tired and ravenous. Even the falling sleet couldn't spoil the sleep their exhausted bodies demanded. But satisfying the aching hunger in their stomachs would be more difficult. They had gone through all their fresh supplies. All that was left was a kind of instant soup Lewis had brought along as emergency rations. It was an emergency but those who ate the vile-tasting liquid refused another helping. The cold and the rocky landscape made hunting game, if there were any to be found, impossible. What would they do for food?

As the men sat pondering this question an animal cry pierced the gathering darkness. It was the same colt that had fallen earlier on the trail. It was hungry, too. Lewis looked around at the tense, wet faces of the men. All turned in the direction of the helpless colt. The captain nodded grimly to his partner. Clark ordered several men to get their knives and follow him. Without speaking a word, they went to where the colt lay in the darkness. Its frightened whinny filled the air once more and then all was silent. Soon the corps feasted on cooked horsemeat.

But Meriwether Lewis could not sleep that night. He knew they could ill afford to kill any more horses. They were counting on the beasts to carry their supplies and other belongings over the mountains. Some other source of food would have to be found if they were not to starve on the trail.

Lewis looked up at the full moon and thought about his friend and mentor, Thomas Jefferson. The President of the United States may have been a brilliant man, but he knew nothing about the true nature of the Rocky Mountains. He had assured Lewis that crossing the mountains would be no more than a brisk, refreshing walk. There would be no troublesome canoes to lug and their horses would carry all their remaining supplies. All the expedition members had to do was walk up one side of the mountains and down the other.

Lewis smiled grimly to himself at their innocence. Of course, Jefferson couldn't be held responsible. Every "authority" on the West had the same illusion. Lewis wished every one of them were with him now, trudging up the steep rocks, drenched to the skin by the sleet and snow. Unable to sleep, Lewis opened his daily journal. By the dim light of the fire, he wrote down his thoughts about the day's experiences. Nearby, another member of the expedition, Patrick Gass, was doing the same. Gass was not an educated man like Lewis, but he experienced the same fears and longings, and he was able to express them in writing. These were, Gass wrote with conviction, "the most terrible mountains I ever beheld."

The next morning Lewis sent Clark out ahead with six hunters to find fresh game. The seven camped along a stream, which Clark appropriately named "Hungry

3

Creek." Their expectations were high, but the only game they found was a stray horse that they killed, butchered, and cooked. They ate some of the horsemeat and left the rest behind for Lewis and the others.

Later, when the ravenous main party found the horsemeat, they devoured it, washing it down with bear oil. When that was gone, they subsisted on a few berries they picked from bushes, and wax candles which they gnawed on.

Clark's group was more fortunate. The day after they killed the stray horse, they found themselves in a valley as different from the mountains as heaven is from earth. The rocks and snow were gone, replaced by gorgeous green trees and fertile grasslands. The gentle valley was inhabited by a people as hospitable as the land seemed to be. These were the Nez Perce Indians, who welcomed Clark and his men with the first fresh food they had eaten in weeks—bread and berries and, best of all, salmon, the fish of the open sea. Could the ocean itself be far away?

The men gorged themselves on the rich bounty and promptly threw most of it up. Their poor, shrunken, empty stomachs couldn't handle it.

Three days later they were joined in their valley retreat by Lewis and the main party. Here, in the friendly Nez Perce village, they recuperated from the terrible mountain journey, and looked forward with anticipation to the last leg of their long trip. Lewis, his strength and confidence regained, ordered new canoes built for the final trek to the sea. After the ordeal of the mountains, the explorers could return to the method of travel they were most used to.

In a few days, the Lewis and Clark expedition would voyage down the Clearwater River, into the twisting Snake River, and finally into the wide, welcoming waters of the Columbia. This mighty river, long shrouded in mystery, would carry the most remarkable journey in American history to its final destination—the vast Pacific Ocean.

2

Two Boys from Virginia

No TWO FIGURES in American history have been so closely linked together as those brave explorers of the West, Meriwether Lewis and William Clark. We grow up learning to say their names in one breath, as if they were two sides of the same person. Richard Dillon, in his biography of Meriwether Lewis, noticed that many of the books about Lewis and Clark have suggested "that these two rugged individualists were Siamese twins of the Western trails."

The truth is that Lewis and Clark, despite their close partnership, were as unlike as two people could be. It is their contrasting personalities that make their friendship so remarkable and the different paths they took after their great adventure so touching. To learn what brought the two men together in the first place, we need to look at the common background that shaped their youth.

The state of Virginia is divided into three main sections—the eastern Tidewater, the central Piedmont, and the western mountains, valleys, and ridges of the Appalachian Mountains. The Tidewater is named for the tidal waters that flow up its numerous rivers and bays. Here in Caroline County on August 1, 1770, William Clark was born to farmer John Clark and his wife Ann Rogers. William was the ninth of ten children. The family lived on a farm near the city of Richmond.

When Clark was four, his eldest brother George returned home from fighting Indians in the Colonial Wars. George Rogers Clark was a larger-than-life hero to his little brother. Already famous as an Indian fighter, he would become one of the greatest generals of the American Revolution. George Clark captured three important British supply bases in what is now Illinois and Indiana, and helped the new republic lay claim to land in the "Northwest Territory" stretching westward to the Mississippi River.

Young William listened eagerly as his big brother told of his experiences living in the wilderness and fighting Indians. He dreamed of having similar adventures. Such dreams were not unrealistic for a spirited boy growing up on the frontier in the 1780s.

When he was fourteen, Clark's family loaded their possessions, their children, and their slaves onto a flatboat and journeyed down the Ohio River to the Kentucky wilderness. At Louisville they were met by George, who helped them clear land for a homestead. William helped, too, to build a cabin and flour mill. He also hunted wild animals for the dinner table.

In 1786, two Indian tribes, the Shawnee and Wabash,

went to war with the Kentucky settlers in a desperate attempt to keep their lands. General George Roger Clark raised an army of a thousand men to fight the tribes. William, now sixteen, begged George to take him along. His brother agreed, and for the next few months Clark received a first-class education in survival and Indian fighting. George taught him how to blaze a trail, make a map, and prepare for an Indian attack.

William Clark came from home from the Indian war with an unquenchable thirst for adventure. In 1792, before his 21st birthday, he joined the United States Army. For six years Clark fought Indians as a soldier, but he learned other skills as well. He mastered the craft of canoemaking and learned how to build a sturdy bridge over a river. He also learned how to survive in the wilderness by living off the land. Once, lost in the forest, he lived for several weeks on blackberries.

Clark's commanding officer for much of his Army service was Major General "Mad" Anthony Wayne. Wayne had earned his strange nickname by his reckless courage in fighting the British during the Revolution. What impressed Clark most about his commanding officer was not his bravery, but his strict sense of discipline. During one long winter with nothing to do, Wayne kept his soldiers busy with target practice, drilling, and marching. This good use of leisure time to prepare one's self for future danger was something Clark wouldn't forget when he himself became a leader of men.

Four years after Clark's birth, Meriwether Lewis was

born on August 18, 1774, in Albermarle County, in Virginia's Piedmont region. Piedmont is a French word meaning "at the foot of the mountains." This rich, fertile farmland lies in the foothills of the stately Blue Ridge Mountains.

The Lewis family owned a sprawling farm named Ivy Creek Plantation. The homestead stood on a gentle slope about seven miles west of the town of Charlottesville. It was named Locust Hill after the noisy insects that lived in the grassy meadows.

When Lewis was a few years old, the American Revolution broke out. His father, William, like hundreds of other patriotic Virginians, went off to fight the British. A brave soldier, William Lewis died of pneumonia while on his way to rejoin his troops in 1779. Meriwether was only five years old. After his father's death, he grew closer to his mother, Lucy, who would remain his close friend for the rest of his life.

Lucy Lewis was a brave and resourceful woman. Her knowledge of herbs and their medicinal properties was extraordinary, and she taught everything she knew to her son. Meriwether learned which herb or root would cure a fever or dysentery, a painful disease of the intestines. This knowledge would help him to be a skillful physician on his famous Western expedition. Lucy also instilled a strong sense of honor and responsibility in Meriwether and his young sister and brother. They grew up with this motto on the family's coat-of-arms as their personal credo: *Omore Solum Forti Patria Est.*

This is Latin for "To the Brave Man, Everything He Does Is for His Country."

The other person to have a profound influence on young Lewis was his nearest neighbor, Thomas Jefferson. Jefferson, already famous as the author of the Declaration of Independence, lived three miles away at his home, which he named Monticello. Thomas Jefferson was a man of great learning and many interests. Besides being a masterful politician and author, he was also an architect, inventor, musician, and scientist. He had a passion for the natural history of his home state, Virginia, and collected minerals, insects, plants, and animals of the region.

Young Meriwether Lewis was in awe of Monticello and its remarkable owner. He visited frequently and was always welcomed by Jefferson, who had no son. The older man would sometimes summon Lewis to Monticello by flashing signals in the sunlight with a looking glass. Lewis quickly became Jefferson's eager student and friend. The two would talk for hours about everything under the sun. Lewis admired Jefferson's mind and imagination, and Jefferson saw himself reflected in the spirited youth's curiosity and ambition. He eventually became almost a father to the growing boy.

At 13, Lewis's more formal education began. Lucy sent him away to school. The following year, she married Captain John Marks, a friend of Jefferson's. She moved to her new husband's estate in Georgia with her two younger children. Lewis, now 14, stayed behind in

11

Virginia to manage his late father's 1,000-acre estate. This might seem like an overwhelming responsibility for one so young, but Lewis, with his Uncle Nicholas's help, did an excellent job of running the family plantation. At 18, he left school to run the estate full time. Like his great teacher, however, he never stopping learning. He read every book he could lay his hands on and collected specimens of local plants and insects that he found on his property.

Tragedy struck the Lewis family a second time when Merriwether's stepfather John Marks, who had been in poor health for years, died in 1792. Young Lewis made the long journey to Georgia to bring home his mother and stepsister Mary. On their way back, an incident occurred that illustrates the courage and quick wits of the young man.

The Lewises stopped with other travelers for supper on the trail and built a campfire for cooking. Nearby Indians saw the light of their fire and prepared to attack the party. While the older men were paralyzed with panic, Meriwether Lewis kept a cool head. He seized a bucket of water and threw it on the fire, extinguishing it. The Indians could no longer see them clearly in the darkness and decided to retreat.

Two years later, a war broke out for which young Lewis quickly volunteered. It was not fought against Indians, but a group of rebellious farmers in western Pennsylvania. These farmers used their corn and rye to make whiskey to earn money. A federal tax was decreed on whiskey and the farmers strongly opposed it.

In the summer of 1794, the farmers took up arms against federal authorities sent to enforce the tax law. This uprising came to be called the Whiskey Rebellion. President George Washington sent troops to put a stop to it. Meriwether Lewis joined the troops and went off to Pennsylvania. The Whiskey Rebellion was quickly put down with hardly a shot fired, but Lewis found his taste of military life to his liking. He stayed on to become a regular Ensign in the United States Army.

It was during this time that he first met the man who would become his close friend and partner in adventure, William Clark. They met in a sharpshooters company and found they shared a love of the rugged outdoor life. Their looks and personalities, however, were worlds apart. Lewis was tall, handsome, with sensitive, fine-chiselled features, fair skin, and dark hair. He was serious, something of an intellectual, moody, introverted, and often quiet around other people. He was never happier than when he was off by himself, tramping through the woods. Today we would call him a "loner."

Clark was just the opposite. He had a round, ruddy face, a stocky build, and bright red hair. He had little schooling and didn't worry too much about anything. Clark was, above all, a cheerful, good-natured fellow who got along well with nearly everyone he met. Despite their differences, or maybe because of them, the two young soldiers became the best of friends. Perhaps each saw in the other traits he would like to have.

For a time Clark was Lewis's superior officer. However, poor health and money problems back home caused him to resign his position on July 1, 1796 and return to Kentucky. Lewis stayed on in the Army. He loved the discipline, the adventure, and constant traveling of military life. In a letter to his mother he admitted that "rambling" was his "governing passion." He was an excellent officer with a natural talent for leadership, and rose quickly in the ranks. He was promoted to lieutenant in 1798 and became a captain in 1800. He was only 26 years old. Lewis's years of experience running the family plantation had made him a sharp businessman, and he was appointed to the job of regimental paymaster, in charge of the regiment's money.

Although their careers had diverged, Lewis and Clark remained good friends. Clark often traveled to Virginia on family business and would always find time to visit Lewis at Locust Hill or his latest Army post.

While Meriwether Lewis was getting on in the Army, his old friend Thomas Jefferson was rising to even greater heights in politics. During Washington's two terms as the country's first president, Jefferson served as his secretary of state. John Adams became president in 1796, but lost in a bid for a second term to Jefferson. In 1801, Thomas Jefferson became the third President of the United States.

Through all these years, Jefferson had not forgotten his young friend from Albermarle County, Meriwether Lewis. When it came time for him to select a private secretary, he could think of no one better suited for the position. In a letter dated February 23, 1801, the President wrote to his friend, "Your knowledge of the Western Country, of the Army, and of all its interests and relations has rendered it desirable for public as well as private purposes that you should be engaged in that office." Jefferson explained that while the salary was low (five hundred dollars a year), Lewis would retain his rank as captain and have few expenses since he would become "one of my family."

It took Lewis only four days to respond. "I . . . with pleasure accept the office, nor were further motives necessary to induce my compliance than that you, Sir, could conceive that in the discharge of the duties of that office I could be serviceable to my Country, or useful to yourself."

Lewis arrived in Washington on April 1. Jefferson had just set off for Monticello and left word for his new secretary to join him there. Little did Lewis dream as he traveled to the President's home that his employer had far greater plans for him than taking dictation and entertaining visiting dignitaries. Jefferson saw Lewis as the one person who could help him fulfill a dream he had cherished for twenty years — a dream that would change the face of the United States forever.

3

A Dream of Empire

THE UNITED STATES in 1801 was a very different
country than it is today. Instead of fifty states,
there were only sixteen — the original thirteen
states plus Vermont, Kentucky, and Tennessee. Brave pioneers were moving westward, finding
new homes and open land in the wilderness beyond the
Appalachian Mountains, but this migration ended at the
Mississippi River. Beyond this, the land was unfamiliar
and believed to be dangerous.

The Far West, from the Rocky Mountains to the Pacific coast, was almost completely unknown. The vast
majority of Americans knew nothing about these vast
"Western lands" and preferred to leave it that way.
Most people knew that the West was filled with fur, timber, and other resources, and wanted the land for that
reason, but it was too dangerous. Trappers and mountain men had dared to travel there to find furs to sell,
but few had returned to tell about it.

Russian and British traders had visited the Pacific
coast and the Spanish had centuries-old settlements in

the Southwest. In general, though, as much as they wanted the goods that were there, most people were afraid of the West. The only other humans to inhabit this large territory were Indians, and most settlers considered them hostile savages. The general attitude of Americans toward the West was summed up by author John Lowell, who claimed the northern part of the West was a vast hostile wilderness "which will not be inhabited by any beings but bears and buffaloes for five hundred years."

There were a few far-sighted Americans who saw the West as more than a wilderness. They believed it was a great region with untold natural resources that could become home for future generations of Americans, once it was settled. They saw the possibilities of the West, not the danger. They wanted to explore the West and claim it for their own. One of these people was Thomas Jefferson. Jefferson dreamed of a Western Empire that would turn the United States into one of the most powerful and richest nations on earth. The West and its wonders were his personal obsession for at least twenty years before he became president. As early as 1783, while still a congressman from Virginia, Jefferson attempted to send an exploring party into the West to find out what was there. He believed that once the region was explored and accurately mapped, people would feel safe in settling there. The West would capture their imagination, just as it had his.

The first person that Jefferson elected to be his "agent of empire" was actually William Clark's big brother,

George. George Rogers Clark, who had helped to win the Kentucky and Tennessee territories for the United States after the Revolution, showed surprisingly little interest in going beyond the Mississippi. He turned down Jefferson's offer and thus lost his chance to become even more famous.

Two years later, while serving as United States Minister to France, Jefferson found a more willing adventurer to carry out his expedition. He was John Ledyard, one of the oddest characters in the history of American exploration. Ledyard was preparing to cross Russia on foot when Jefferson met him. With a little encouragement from the American minister, Ledyard agreed to extend his solo journey across the Pacific by boat and into the American Northwest. Unfortunately, he never got all the way across Russia. He was arrested by Russian soldiers under order from their queen, Catherine the Great, and escorted to the Polish border.

Another seven years would pass before Jefferson would again try to implement his "dream journey." This time he would be better organized. In 1792, as secretary of state under George Washington, he received the financial backing of the American Philosophical Society in Philadelphia, of which he was a ranking member. That same year, American sailor Robert Gray had discovered the mouth of the Columbia River while sailing around the globe. The Columbia flows into the North Pacific near the border of present-day Oregon and Washington state.

Jefferson saw the Columbia as a possible waterway

across the continent from the Mississippi that would provide a profitable route for trade from the Atlantic to the Pacific. No one knew, however, how far the Columbia extended or if anyone could sail its entire length. Jefferson saw his Western expedition as an opportunity to find out about this valuable waterway. Among the men who applied to be part of the expedition was 18-year-old Meriwether Lewis. Jefferson, at the time, felt his friend was too young and inexperienced and turned him down. The man he finally settled on to lead the expedition was a French botanist, Andre Michaux. Not long after Michaux set off Jefferson learned, to his horror, that Michaux was a secret agent in the employ of the French government. Under the American flag, Michaux would be exploring the Western territory for a foreign power! Jefferson quickly recalled the expedition before it got any further than Kentucky.

The French were not the only European power with a stake in the West. Spain officially owned all of the land west of the Mississippi. The Mississippi Valley region, known at that time as Louisiana, had been the property of the French since its discovery by French explorer Sieur de la Salle in 1682. In 1762, King Louis XV of France gave all of Louisiana, including its capital and main port, New Orleans, to his cousin King Charles III of Spain. It remained under Spanish rule until 1800.

By this time, France had emerged from a bloody revolution with a new leader. Napoleon Bonaparte had his own ambitions of building an American Empire. Spain's days of colonial glory were coming to an end and the bold Napoleon took advantage of the weaker nation. In 1800, he negotiated a secret treaty with Spain that returned all the Louisiana Territory to France. The United States had previously had an agreement with Spain that allowed American ships to travel down the Mississippi River to the port of New Orleans. When the secret deal with France leaked out, Jefferson, who was about to become president, feared that France would close New Orleans off to the United States and end a valuable trade route. In November 1802, this is exactly what happened. The Spanish Intendant at New Orleans, still officially in charge, withdrew permission to the United States to store goods there for shipment abroad.

Jefferson immediately attempted to buy New Orleans from the French. He told the American Minister to France, Robert Livingston, to start negotiations with Napoleon. Then he sent Secretary of State James Monroe over to seal the deal. The timing was perfect for the United States. Napoleon had just suffered a humiliating defeat in the French West Indian island colony of Hispaniola, where black revolutionary Toussaint L'Ouverture had wiped out the French troops sent to suppress his revolution. Napoleon's enthusiasm for an American Empire was seriously dampened. Furthermore, he needed money to keep his war with Great Britain going.

Livingston met with the French foreign minister and made an offer for New Orleans and the Floridas, previously owned by Spain. To Livingston's shock, the minister asked what the Americans were willing to offer for *all* of the Louisiana Territory. Monroe and Livingston, knowing Jefferson would approve of the purchase, went ahead, without taking the time to consult with the president.

The Louisiana Purchase has been called by historians the biggest real estate bargain in history. The United States bought 830,000 square miles of land for $15 million. That works out to less than 3 cents an acre. The treaty that finalized the sale was signed on May 2, 1803. Word of it didn't reach Washington until July 14. But Jefferson, who was thrilled at the news, hadn't waited for the purchase to make his exploration of the West legal.

Six months earlier, he had already secretly asked Congress for money to back a westward expedition. Knowing that many conservative members of Congress were opposed to Western expansion, he reassured them that the expedition would be a harmless "literary mission." Its goals would be to study the plants, animals, and minerals in the region, make friends with the Indians, and search for a waterway to the Pacific "for the purpose of extending the external trade of the United States." No one could raise any serious objections to this proposal, and Congress granted Jefferson the modest sum of $2,500 for his expedition. They also approved his choice for leader of the exploring party — his private secretary, Meriwether Lewis.

Lewis had most of the requirements Jefferson was looking for in his agent of empire. He was young, strong, a military man, intelligent, and a good leader. Although not a trained scientist, Lewis had a strong interest in natural history and he now underwent a crash course in all the sciences. Jefferson had him tutored by the most learned men of science he could find, including a physician. Since there would be no doctor on the expedition, Lewis would have to fill out his medical knowledge as well.

The President and his secretary discussed and planned the expedition throughout 1802, often at Monticello. There, in familiar surroundings, they would settle down in Jefferson's study and pore over maps of the West as they planned their dream journey. They decided to call it the Corps of Discovery. Oddly enough, the 60-year-old Jefferson had never been further west than Stauton, Virginia and would never see the wonders his young friend experienced. But in his imagination, Jefferson went to the Pacific and back many times. Lewis would be his eyes and ears, writing down everything he saw and experienced. He would also collect specimens of wildlife and minerals and send them back to the President for his collection.

The route Lewis would take west was simple and straightforward. He set out in the spring from St. Louis, the last outpost of civilization, and then sail up to 300 miles along the Missouri River before winter set in. The expedition would camp for the winter, then resume travel in the spring, cross the Rocky Mountains, and reach the Pacific Ocean by late summer or early autumn. Both men hoped that a return trip overland would be unnecessary. After all, there were British and American ships anchored regularly at the mouth of the Columbia River. Jefferson gave Lewis an extraordinary letter, a kind of blank check from the United States government, that would get him and his men free passage back to the East Coast on the first ship they sighted offshore.

With the plan set, they had to decide how many men would be needed for the expedition. Both agreed that fifteen would be sufficient for the journey. In fact, they ended up with over twice that number, including an Indian woman and her baby. Lewis realized the first person he had to recruit was a reliable second-in-command. This man would have to be as resourceful as himself and someone he could trust completely. His first choice was his old Army companion, William Clark. Besides being a good friend, Clark had other assets as well. He was an excellent navigator and a skilled map maker.

Lewis wrote to his friend on June 19, 1803. Besides offering Clark a job, he asked him to help recruit volunteers for the expedition. Lewis was looking for "some good hunters, stout, healthy, unmarried men, accustomed to the woods, and capable of bearing bodily fatigue in a pretty considerable degree." Weeks went by and no reply came from Clark. Lewis was worried he'd have to find someone else, but he waited nervously. He kept himself busy for the moment with preparations for the long journey.

At the government arsenal in Harper's Ferry, West Virginia, Lewis gathered the weapons they would need to protect themselves and to hunt for wild game. These included rifles, pistols, and gunpowder packed in waterproof lead canisters, as well as knives and toma-hawks. In Lancaster, Pennsylvania Lewis bought scientific equipment for surveying land and observing the stars and planets. A major part of the budget, over $600, went for gifts for the Indians they would encoun-ter — everything from scissors and mirrors to beads and bells.

With most of the supplies ready, Lewis set forth from Washington on July 4, 1803. He was so anxious to get started that he forgot his horse's bridle, his dagger, and pocketbook. Jefferson had the last two items mailed to him. Lewis arrived in Pittsburgh, Pennsylvania where the expedition's main water transportation, a large, flat-bottomed boat, was to be waiting for him. Two disap-pointments greeted him on his arrival. The boat was not finished, and there was still no word from Clark. To have his boat completed, the impatient Lewis threat-ened and browbeat the careless boat builder, who was more fond of alcohol than work. Sadly, he also sent word to a Lieutenant Moses Hook, who was second choice for his right-hand man. Then, on July 29, Clark's long-awaited reply arrived. "I will cheerfully join you, my friend," he wrote. "I do assure you that no man lives with whom I would prefer to undertake such a trip as yourself . . . . I join you with head and heart."

Lewis promised a captain's commission to his friend, but the War Department refused to give Clark a rank above that of a second lieutenant. Lewis never breathed a word to the men about this. No one on the expedition except for Lewis and Clark believed the two men to be

William Clark, co-leader of the Corps of Discovery. Although technically a lower rank than his friend Meriwether Lewis, he was treated as a co-captain by Lewis and the rest of the party. Without his leadership and navigational skills, the expedition might never have survived.

anything but equals, co-captains of the Corps of Discovery. No greater proof could be found of their close friendship.

By late August the keel boat was finally finished. It was nearly 55 feet long and could be rowed, sailed, or poled like a raft, depending on river conditions. On August 31, Lewis, accompanied by ten recruits, a boat pilot, and his dog Scammon, pushed off from Pittsburgh and down the Ohio River. They stopped at Louisville to pick up Clark, his black servant York, and several more men. Their first destination was St. Louis. The great adventure had begun.

4

Into the Wilderness

I N 1803, St. Louis was a tiny trading post on the west bank of the Mississippi River, ten miles south of where the Missouri River joins the Mississippi. The settlement was founded forty years earlier by a French fur trader, Pierre Laclede Liquest and his 14-year-old stepson. Even though the land was owned by Spain, the post was mostly settled by French pioneers who preferred the easy-going rule of the Spaniards to the stricter British, who owned the land just east of the Mississippi. The land under British rule became American territory following the Revolutionary War, while St. Louis remained Spanish.

Lewis and Clark arrived in St. Louis on December 8, and were greeted by Spanish Lieutenant Governor Don Carlos Duhault Delassus. Delassus wished Lewis well and wrote to his superiors in Spain that the expedition was a harmless one. He praised "Captain Merry Whether" as a "very well educated man, and of many talents." The Spanish government, however, did not agree with Delassus's assessment, and feared Lewis and Clark might change their route and head south to attack the Spanish colonial capital of Santa Fe in present-day New Mexico. A band of Spanish soldiers was dispatched from Santa Fe to drive back the explorers. Fortunately, the soldiers themselves were forced back by hostile Indians and never posed a threat to the Corps of Discovery.

Meanwhile, Lewis had no intention of leaving St. Louis before spring. It would be foolhardy to set out in winter with its numbing cold and snow, he decided. Besides, the Missouri, their main means of travel, would soon be frozen solid until spring. The captains also needed time to complete stocking the expedition and to recruit and train more men.

The men built a winter camp at Wood River a few miles above St. Louis across from the mouth of the Missouri. For the next five months they kept busy drilling, building two more boats, and doing other chores. Six more soldiers and nine French boatmen were recruited. The party now numbered over forty. It was a curious mix of soldiers, civilians, hunters, boatmen, and translators. It was a youthful group, ranging in age from 18 to 33. Clark was the oldest member; Lewis was 29.

Many of the men were picked for their range of abilities. George Drouillard, for instance, was not only the chief hunter but was also an experienced scout and Indian interpreter. Since his name was pronounced "Drewyer," both Lewis and Clark usually spelled it that way. Other key members of the expedition were Sergeant John Ordway, third in command, and Private

Pierre Cruzatte, a one-eyed Creole who was head boatman. Nicknamed "St. Peter," Cruzatte had another talent that would make him one of the most popular members of the expedition. He was an expert fiddler and kept the men entertained and in good spirits with his music.

Then there were the famous "nine young men from Kentucky," as they came to be called. Each was an expert marksman and kept the company well supplied with fresh meat. This group included future mountain man John Colter, whose reputation would one day be nearly as legendary as those of Lewis and Clark. The most curious member of the party was York, the family servant of the Clark family, who was almost certainly a slave. Dedicated to his master, York was a giant of a man, whose great strength would be useful in the rough times ahead. He also had a great sense of humor and a ready wit.

Provisions for the long journey were kept to the basics. Lewis and Clark counted on living off what they could find along their route as much as possible. They filled the keel boat with fifty barrels of salt pork, twenty barrels of flour, fourteen barrels of corn meal, and smaller amounts of salt, sugar, biscuits, coffee, and dried apples. For drinking, there were thirty gallons of whiskey. In those times, alcohol was as common a beverage as water, coffee, or soda is today. Even at that, Lewis was careful to dole out the whiskey sparingly. He rewarded the men with it at the end of a hard day or to celebrate a holiday.

March 9, 1804 was truly a day worth celebrating. On that day the Louisiana Territory officially became part of the United States. The ceremony, in which the French turned over the territory to the Americans, took place at the old Government House in St. Louis. Lewis acted as aide to Captain Amos Stoddard, the Army officer authorized to accept the territory, and was also the President's personal envoy. Cannons boomed and rifles fired salutes as the proper papers were signed by both sides. Two days later, the American flag was raised over the Government House.

Lewis and Clark could now proceed on their expedition across land that for the most part belonged to the United States. This was not true of the Oregon Territory, to which no country yet had a claim. The British, who had taken Canada away from the French, were eyeing Oregon and its profitable fur trade. So were the Russians who had trading posts on the Pacific coast. By reaching Oregon, Lewis and Clark hoped to strengthen the United States' claim to this rich, fertile region.

By May the ice on the Missouri was all but melted. At four p.m. on the 14th day of the month, the Corps of Discovery made its grand start into the wilderness, or as the French map makers called it, "Le Pays Inconnu," "the Unknown Land. Clark was in charge of the big keel boat, which served as the flagship and was armed with a cannon. With the two smaller flatboats in tow, they pushed off across the Mississippi and into the muddy, rolling waters of the Missouri. They would not lay eyes on St. Louis again for almost two and a half years.

The voyage got off to a good start. The river, while twisting and unpredictable, was mostly cooperative. The men marvelled at the silent, dense forests they passed along the shore and the spectacular sunsets in the western skies. The Missouri proved to be a bountiful source of fresh food. The men caught pike, bass, perch, trout, and catfish, as well as mussels and shrimp. One catfish they caught weighed 128 pounds!

Danger and hardship soon tempered their opinion of the wilderness. On May 23, they stopped to explore a cave whose walls were covered with Indian pictographs. While climbing the rocks above the cave, Lewis lost his balance and slipped over a 300-foot cliff. He narrowly escaped death by catching hold of a ledge twenty feet below. It was only the first of many narrow escapes for the accident-prone explorer.

The following day they entered the last civilized outpost on the Missouri, La Charrette. The settlement's most famous resident was the still spry 70-year-old Daniel Boone, but the explorers had no idea Boone lived there and so these three great Western legends never met.

Back on the river, the men found the insects a constant irritant. To keep off the mosquitoes and ticks, they smeared their sunburned bodies with cooking grease. They found no such protection, however, from boils and dysentery.

While most of the men endured these hardships with discipline and good spirits, a few needed close watching. Lewis, while fair, was a strict disciplinarian. Those who broke regulations received swift punishment. When one man was caught stealing a keg of whiskey, he was punished with fifty lashes of a whip. While this may seem cruel and unusual punishment to us today, it was common practice at the time, especially in the military.

On June 12, the explorers crossed bows with a French fur raft headed for St. Louis. The traders warned the party about some Sioux Indians they might soon meet, calling them thieves and liars that were not to be trusted. The Frenchmen spoke better of the Mandans, a more peaceful and friendly tribe.

Both Lewis and Clark were fascinated by Indians and looked forward to meeting all of the many tribes that inhabited the land ahead. Although both men had fought Indians before, they had a deep respect for these Native Americans. Clark was especially knowledgeable about the Indians and their culture. The only Indians they had seen in the first 600 miles of their trek were a few Kickapoos. Finally, on August 2, they met a formal delegation of two tribes — the Missouri and Oto Indians. The following day Lewis and Clark sat down with their interpreters for a powwow with six chiefs representing both tribes.

This first encounter would set a pattern for their future councils with Indian leaders. After passing the peace pipe in silence, Lewis launched into a long, prepared speech in which he explained to the Indians that they now were living under the protection of their "new Great Father Jefferson of the 17 Great Nations." He told

34

them their expedition was a peaceful one of exploration and that other white men with goods to trade would follow them in the future. He urged the Indians to make peace with their tribal enemies. "Children, do these things which your Great Father advises and be happy," he concluded. "Avoid the councils of bad birds, turn on your heels from them as you would from the precipice of a high rock, whose summit reached the clouds and whose base was washed by the gulf of human woes, lest by one false step you should bring upon your nation the displeasure of your Great Father . . . who would consume you as the fire consumes the grass of the plains . . . . But it is not [his] wish . . . to injure you; on the contrary, he is now pursuing the measures best calculated to insure your happiness."

Lewis urged an absent head chief to come visit Jefferson in Washington, an invitation he would extend to nearly every tribe they would come in contact with. The Indian chiefs replied to Lewis's speech with one of their own, just as long and just as solemnly delivered. Then, to the delight of the Indians the captains distributed the gifts they had brought. They saved the best presents, such as medals, military jackets, and cocked hats for the chiefs. Lewis ended the council with a demonstration of his prized weapon, a Harrison air gun he had bought especially for the expedition. The Indians stared in amazement as he fired the rifle, which unlike other firearms of the day did not need reloading. It was an effective show of strength and a subtle warning that the Indians had better not attempt to harm them during their stay. Lewis and Clark named the site of this first powwow Council Bluff. It lies fifteen miles north of what is now Omaha, Nebraska.

Along with the Indians, the explorers discovered some new and fascinating animals. On July 3, they sighted their first beaver pond. Drouillard was so taken with the furry, flat-tailed creatures that he adopted one as a pet. Lewis was more impressed by the long-clawed badger. He had one animal skinned and its pelt tanned to send back East to the President. Lewis was a scrupulous observer of the wildlife and natural landscape around him. Both he and Clark kept journals which they wrote in nearly every day, and encouraged other members of the expedition to do the same. At least five of them did so, leading one historian to call the men of the Corps of Discovery, "the writingest explorers of their time."

Soon the two captains began to take on different tasks. Lewis would scout ahead along the shore accompanied by Scammon, his Newfoundland dog. Clark, the better navigator, stayed with the boats on the river. Lewis relished tramping through the wilderness, taking endless notes on every plant, mineral, and stream he came across. He was never happier than when off by himself. Other people often made him nervous and sometimes depressed. Even in the wilderness, with a small group of similarly adventurous companions, Lewis remained ever the loner.

The more sociable Clark kept the men in line. As time went on, Lewis roamed farther and farther ahead of the boats. Sometimes he would get a full day ahead of the others and camp out on the riverbank with nothing but a small fire for warmth and the cold ground for a bed. Then he would wait for the boats' arrival in the morning.

Not everyone in the party was enjoying the expedition as much as Lewis. Private Moses B. Reed was caught attempting to desert in Indian country. After receiving his corporal punishment, Reed was stripped of his rank and treated by the rest of the party as a common laborer for the remainder of his time among them.

After one powwow with Indians, Cruzatte brought out his fiddle and the men danced to the happy music. The Indians, who had no musical instruments of their own, were as delighted watching and listening as children. The only one who didn't appreciate the fiddler's art was Scammon. He covered his ears and moaned mournfully at the high-pitched sounds.

The most enthusiastic dancer was Sergeant Charles Floyd, a young Irishman. When the dancing ended, though, Floyd collapsed with a fever. During the night he began vomiting. The next morning he was even worse. Lewis attempted to treat him with herbs and medicine, but to no avail. Within hours, to the shock of the entire company, the poor man died. Clark called Floyd's illness "bilious colic," but modern doctors, reviewing the symptoms, believe Floyd may have died from a burst appendix. If this is true, there was nothing Lewis or any physician of the time could have done to save him. The art of surgery had not yet developed enough to treat that successfully.

They buried their companion on a slope and marked his grave with a cedar post. The captains named the spot Floyd's Bluff, the name it bears to this day. Charles Floyd had the dubious distinction of being the first American soldier to die west of the Mississippi River. He was the first and only member of the Corps of Discovery to lose his life on the expedition. It is a tribute to the responsible leadership of Lewis and Clark that despite all the dangers they would face in the next two years, they brought every other member of their party home safe and sound.

On August 18, Lewis silently observed his 30th birthday. By the end of the month they would be deep in Sioux country and have their first unfriendly encounter with Indians.

5

Indians — Friendly and Hostile

SIOUX MEANS "ENEMY" in the Indians' native tongue. The name was well-chosen, for few of the known Western tribes were more warlike than the Sioux. While hostile to Americans who ventured into their territory, the tribe was friendly with British traders, who supplied them with muskets and gunpowder. If the British and Americans were to go to war again, there was no doubt whose side the Sioux would be on. President Jefferson viewed this situation with alarm and gave Lewis explicit instructions to try to improve relations with the Sioux while avoiding any confrontation with them. This would be a very difficult task.

The Sioux, like many large Indian tribes, was actually made up of many small tribes that were collectively called a "nation." The first tribe of the Sioux Nation the explorers encountered were the Yankton Sioux. These Indians, to the captains' relief, were peaceful and easygoing. While they didn't seem particularly interested in

Lewis's set speech, they listened patiently and later accepted the gifts with enthusiasm.

On September 25, the party met with the Teton Sioux, a larger, more powerful tribe. Lewis took great pains to show them the white men's might in order to avoid any trouble. He and Clark dressed in their military uniforms, which they rarely wore on the river, and came on shore accompanied by the soldier members of the expedition. The soldiers paraded back and forth along the riverbank as the Indians arrived for their powwow with the white men. The American flag was raised on a pole and snapped boldly in the breeze.

The Sioux were dressed in deerskin robes and full-feathered headdresses. Some carried muskets — an ominous sign. Black Buffalo, the head chief, gave the signal for the other braves to sit and Lewis delivered his speech. Afterwards, the captains distributed their gifts. Everything seemed to be going smoothly. Then Lewis invited Black Buffalo and the other chiefs to come on board the keel boat. This proved to be a serious mistake. Lewis's second mistake was to offer whiskey to the Indians on board the boat as a sign of friendship. One chief, named the Partisan, began to act boisterous and ugly. Whether this was a result of the whiskey or Partisan just using the alcohol as an excuse to act up, neither captain could tell for certain.

The tension grew and finally Lewis suggested it was time for the Indians to return to shore. They didn't seem to want to leave, but put up no resistance. Clark got the chiefs into one of the dugout boats, called a pirogue, and steered for shore. Later Clark wrote in his journal, "As soon as I landed the pirogue . . . the Chief's soldiers hugged the mast and the Second Chief [the Partisan] was very insolent both in words and justures [sic]. He pretended drunkenness and staggered up against me, declaring I should not go on, stating he had not received presents sufficient from us."

Clark responded by drawing his sword. Lewis, back on the keel boat, realized something was wrong and ordered the cannon to be manned. Clark told the Partisan that the remainder of their presents had to be saved for the other tribes they would meet on their journey. For a few tense moments no one moved. Then the Sioux, surprised by the firm resistance of the whites, let go of the pirogue. Clark sent the men who had accompanied him back to the main boat and bravely remained behind, surrounded by the Indians.

As Lewis watched nervously, Clark offered his hand in friendship to the chiefs, who refused to take it. When the pirogue returned to the keel boat, Lewis ordered twelve armed men to return in it to the shore. Summoning up every ounce of courage, Clark turned his back on the Indians and strode to the water's edge to meet the returning pirogue. The Partisan sneered, but made no move towards Clark. Then suddenly Black Buffalo and another chief rushed down to the water towards Clark and the arriving pirogue. Lewis was about to give the order for his men to fire, when he realized the two chiefs were not attacking Clark, but talking earnestly to him. They were asking his partner to let them return

41

to the keel boat once more. Clark allowed them aboard, and they formally offered their apologies to the two captains. Lewis took no further chances with the Sioux's unpredictable nature, however. He had the boats moved a mile up the river and anchored off a small island. Clark aptly named it "Bad Humored Island."

The following day the Sioux tried to make up for their bad behavior by inviting the explorers to another pow-wow, but once again troubled flared up. Several braves demanded more tobocco from the explorers for their peace pipes, and a fight was narrowly averted. The entire company heaved a sigh of relief a few days later when they departed from the Tetons' territory. Word of their show of strength soon spread among the other tribes further west. In the future, few Indians would attempt to get the better of the Corps of Discovery.

The next sign of trouble came not from Indians, but one of the group's own number. Private John Newman, tired of the hardships and discipline of the expedition, grumbled to his companions and tried to organize a mutiny. Word of the mutiny got back to the captains, and Newman was court-martialled and found guilty of insubordination. He was sentenced to 75 lashes of the whip. A local Sioux Indian chief who witnessed the whipping was horrified. He told Lewis that his tribe would not expose even a naughty child to such public humiliation. A man found guilty of a serious crime might be killed, but never punished in such a humiliating manner, he explained. Newman, like Private Reed, was demoted to a common laborer. Unlike Reed, Newman would later try to make amends for his crime and be accepted back into the expedition as an equal member.

By October, the expedition was deep in what is now the state of North Dakota. On the 21st, the first snows of winter fell. The captains knew it was time to halt their journey and find a suitable place to wait out the long winter. Fortunately, they didn't have to look far. That very day they met members of a tribe that was as friendly as the Teton Sioux had been hostile. These were the Mandans, a peaceful tribe who welcomed the explorers with open arms. While naturally sociable, the Mandans did have a secret motive for wanting the white men's company. They hoped Lewis and Clark would protect them from their enemies — the Sioux.

The captains immediately began to look for a site to set up a winter camp along the river. On October 30, while scouting the area, Lewis met an important Mandan chief who would have a profound effect on his life, long after the expedition. His name was Sha-ha-ka, which in the Mandan language means "Big White." Big White lived up to his name. He was large and extremely light-skinned for an Indian. With Big White's help, the captains found the perfect site for their headquarters on the east bank of the Missouri.

The men cut down trees and constructed a modest fort, which they named Fort Mandan after their gracious hosts. Fort Mandan consisted of eight crude log cabins surrounded by eight-foot high walls. It was not much of a defense by any standards, but it held the distinction of being the westernmost military outpost in the

43

United States. One Canadian trader was so impressed by the sight of the structure that he wrote it was "so strong as to be almost cannonball proof."

The explorers made good use of the five months of leisure that stretched before them. The hunters kept busy stalking game in the snowy wilderness. The craftsmen built new canoes and made clothing and moccasins. New, heavy clothing was a necessity. The North Dakota winter was a bitter one. The temperature during the night sometimes dipped as low as 45 degrees below zero! Frostbite was an ever-present danger. Each man spent only a half hour at a time on guard duty to prevent his feet from freezing.

The busiest ones of all, not surprisingly, were the two leaders. While Clark made maps and drew pictures of the Indians and wildlife, Lewis kept scientific records of everything from the movement of the ice on the river to temperature changes. He collected and mounted specimens of animals and rocks for the President. By winter's end he had five boxes filled with stuffed animals — prairie dogs, magpies, and prairie hens among them. In his spare time, Lewis worked on a dictionary of the Mandan tongue.

The person who most enjoyed his stay at Fort Mandan was York, Clark's servant. The Indians had never seen a black man before and thought at first he was a white man who had been painted black. At each Mandan village, braves would surround the big, black man. Then one of them, often a chief, would stride up to York, rub some spit between two fingers, and try to wipe the

The Corps of Discovery among the Mandans. This friendly tribe welcomed the expedition, and helped them survive the deadly North Dakota winter. They had never seen a black man before, though, and tried to rub the color off of York, Clark's servant.

paint off his skin. When the black didn't come off, the Indians knew York was genuine.

Instead of being offended by this treatment, York enjoyed it to the fullest and played right along. He convinced the Indians that he was more animal than human by baring his teeth, rolling his eyes and making animal-like noises. The Mandan women found him fascinating. They lined up to kiss York and run their fingers through his black, woolly hair. Their husbands didn't mind any of this. In fact, they encouraged it. It was a Mandan custom to share wives with honored visitors, and no visitor was more honored that winter than York.

During the winter, Lewis and Clark recruited two new members for their mission, one of whom would become the most renowned member of the expedition after themselves. Toussaint Charbonneau was a French-Canadian trapper and fur trader in his mid-forties, who had no special skills to make him especially useful to the explorers. He was no great hunter and later proved to be a disastrous boatman. However, Charbonneau had lived five years among the nearby Hidatsas Indians and knew several Indian languages. Lewis decided they could use his skills as an interpreter and signed him on.

Charbonneau had a young Indian wife named Sacajawea (SACK-uh-ja-WAY-uh), which means "Bird Woman." Although only 17, Sacajawea had had a hard life. A member of the Shoshone tribe, she had been kidnapped at age 12 by the Minnetarees, an enemy tribe. Later, Charbonneau won her from her captors in a gambling game. Lewis was reluctant to have a woman on the expedition, especially when he found out that Sacajawea was eight months pregnant. On the other hand, the party would soon be entering Shoshone country, and her knowledge of the Indians and their language could be very useful. The captains decided Charbonneau's Indian woman could stay.

Christmas 1804 was a day of great celebration for the explorers. They had traveled 1,300 miles and were in good health and spirits. They hoisted the American flag and saluted it with a booming round from the cannon on the keel boat. The day was passed pleasantly with drinking, feasting, and dancing. Cruzatte and his fiddle got a long workout. New Year's Day was just as memorable. The men square danced in one Indian lodge after another, and Cruzatte's fiddle was helped by a tambourine and a tin trumpet.

On February 11, Sacajawea's time had come. Lewis, who had cured snakebites and amputated frostbitten toes, was a bit nervous about delivering his first baby. An old Frenchman, Rene Jesseaume, who had lived for years among the Mandans, suggested Lewis use the powdered rattle of a rattlesnake to hasten the child's birth. Lewis tried the old Indian remedy and the baby, a healthy boy, was delivered without any problem. Charbonneau and Sacajewea named their son Jean Baptiste. He would become one of the best-traveled babies in the West over the next two years.

By the end of March the ice had melted on the river and the explorers were ready to bid farewell to Fort

Mandan and their hosts. They also said good-bye to their main boat. The keel boat headed south for St. Louis. On board were the boxes with the animal specimens for Jefferson, the two court-martialled men, and an Arikara chief, Black Raven, who had taken up Lewis's invitation to visit the "Great White Father" in Washington. Newman, who had done his best to mend his ways, pleaded with Lewis to let him stay with the expedition, but the captain would not be swayed. Although he was moved by Newman's sincerity, he felt he couldn't take a chance on the young soldier causing trouble a second time.

On April 7, 1805, the main party pushed up the Missouri in two pirogues and six canoes. The expedition now numbered 31 men, one woman, and a baby. Lewis wrote these words in his journal: "We were now about to penetrate a country at least 2,000 miles in width, on which the feet of civilized men had never trodden . . . ." Ahead of them lay more wonders — and dangers — than even Thomas Jefferson could have imagined.

6

Savage Bears and Stampeding Buffalo

WHEN PRESIDENT JEFFERSON was giving Lewis his orders for the expedition, he told him to be on the lookout for prehistoric creatures, including dinosaurs and woolly mammoths, thought to still be alive in the Western wilderness. The Corps of Discovery found no such monsters in the West, but they did come up against a more modern beast nearly as fearsome. It was *Ursus (arctos) horribilis*, or by its more common name, the great grizzly bear.

The grizzly was then, and remains today, the king of western North Americans bears. Distinguished by a hump on its shaggy shoulders, the adult grizzly can grows to eight feet in length and weigh up to 500 pounds. Its name comes from the white or silver-tipped coarse outer hairs of its fur that give it a grizzled or grayish appearance.

Before Lewis and Clark, few white men had ever seen a grizzly. The Indians knew the beast well and had a deep fear and respect for its savage strength. Some tribes considered the bear a god with supernatural powers. They would not hunt grizzlies unless one had killed a member of their tribe; then, a band of warriors would track down the mighty animal, being careful to apologize to it before taking its life.

On April 26, 1805, the Corps of Discovery reached the point where the Missouri and Yellowstone Rivers flowed together in what is now Montana. Three days later they came face-to-face with their first grizzlies. Two of the bears surprised several of the men while they were inspecting their trap lines and chased them into camp. Lewis and George Drouillard loaded up their rifles and went in pursuit of the animals. Without warning, the bears rushed at the armed men from behind a clump of trees. The men fired. One bear dropped. The other, wounded, raised its massive head and charged madly towards Lewis. The beast, Lewis later wrote in his journal, "pursued me seventy or eighty yards but, fortunately, had been so badly wounded that he was unable to pursue so closely as to prevent my [reloading] my gun. We again repeated our fire and killed him." A week later, hunters killed a 600-pound male grizzly, but only after firing ten shots into it.

The explorers again met a grizzly on May 12. Lewis was walking along the shore when he was surprised to see William Bratton running towards him, panting and out of breath. Bratton collapsed at Lewis's feet and gasped that he had just shot a grizzly and the wounded animal had chased him for half a mile. Fearing the grizzly might charge the camp, Lewis gathered his seven best hunters and set off to track down the wounded beast. They followed the bear's bloody trail for a mile, and finally found it "perfectly alive" and hidden in the thick brush. The grizzly, sensing death was near, had clawed itself a shallow grave measuring two feet deep and five feet long. The hunters fired two bullets into the animal's skull, killing it instantly. Later Lewis examined the carcass and was surprised to discover that Bratton's bullet had gone clean through the bear's lung. "These bears, being so hard to die, rather intimidate us all," the captain later wrote, adding that he'd rather face "two Indians than one bear."

Lewis's most dangerous encounter with the deadly bears came a month later. He was hunting buffalo and had shot one in a herd, when he turned and saw an enormous grizzly rushing towards him. In an instant, the hunter had become the hunted. Lewis raised his rifle to fire and then realized he hadn't reloaded. He turned and ran for his life. The grizzly followed in swift pursuit. After running eighty yards, Lewis turned to see the grizzly gaining on him. The river lay directly ahead. Without further thought, the explorer plunged into the icy water until it reached his waist. Then he turned with his spontoon, a kind of frontier spear, ready to do battle with the beast. But the bear had no love of water and stopped at the river's edge. After some very tense moments, the grizzly turned and shuffled away.

Next to the grizzly, no animal fascinated the explorers more than the buffalo. They were astonished not so much by the buffalo's size and shape, as by its vast numbers. It has been estimated that over fifty million buffalo roamed North America at the time of Lewis and Clark. Enormous herds darkened the plains in every direction. At times, the men found themselves literally having to push their way through a herd of buffalo. Many of the huge beasts had never seen men before and had no fear of them.

This made the animals easy prey for the hunters. The company feasted on buffalo humps, the tastiest cut of meat, as well as deer steaks, beaver tails, and elk and antelope meat. Every 24 hours, they consumed one buffalo, or four deer, or an elk and a deer. One of Lewis's favorite dishes was a sausage Charbonneau concocted called White Pudding. It was made of a buffalo's intestines stuffed with a mixture of suet, chopped meat, salt, pepper, and flour. All this was boiled and then fried in bear fat until it turned brown.

At a place known as Ash Rapids, Lewis learned a clever trick the Indians used to catch and kill buffalo. The captain climbed a rocky pass by the river to investigate the source of a terrible stench. He came upon a pack of lazy, fat wolves who were so content he had to pick his way through them. One wolf snarled at him, and Lewis drove his spontoon through its bloated belly, killing it. The other wolves paid no attention, but went right on eating. Climbing a steep cliff, Lewis looked down on the source of the smell and the wolves' bounty. At the cliff's base was literally a mountain of buffalo carcasses. "The water appeared to have washed away a part of the immense pile of slaughter and still there remained the fragments of at least a hundred carcasses," he noted.

The Indians later explained to him that they deliberately stampeded herds of buffalo over the cliff as a quick, easy means of killing them. A young brave, dressed in a buffalo robe and holding a buffalo head on the end of a stick, would lie in wait in a hiding place near the cliff's edge. As the herd approached, he would leap up and run toward to cliff's edge. The panic-stricken herd would then follow the decoy to their doom. The decoy, if lucky and fast enough, would duck back into his hiding place. If he wasn't so lucky, he would be either trampled to death by the stampeding herd or pushed over the cliff with them. Since the buffalo's graveyard was often far from the Indians' village, the warriors only took away the choice humps with them and left the rest of the carcasses for the wolves to devour. Lewis fittingly named the nearby stream "Slaughter River."

Once a single buffalo nearly wreaked havoc in the explorers' camp. During the night of May 28, while the camp slept, a buffalo bull dashed headlong through the camp, barely missing the sleeping men and nearly charging right into the tent where Lewis and Clark slept. "When he came near the tent," Lewis later recalled, "my dog saved us by causing him to change his coarse a second time, which he did turning a little to the right, and was quickly out of sight, leaving us, by this time, all in an uproar, with our guns in our hands." It would be one of their last encounters with buffalo until their return journey, but it was certainly a memorable one.

A different kind of disaster had occurred earlier that month on the river. Charbonneau was aboard one of the pirogues that contained important papers and scientific instruments. A poor navigator who couldn't even swim, the Canadian was straggling behind the other boats when a sudden windstorm sent him into a panic. Cruzatte, who was in the bow of the boat, ordered Charbonneau to grab the rudder to steady the foundering vessel. But Charbonneau, afraid the rudder would swing around and knock him overboard, did nothing. Cruzatte threatened to shoot the cringing man if he didn't follow his orders, and Charbonneau finally reached for the rudder. He was too late. The pirogue tipped violently to one side, dumping its precious cargo into the churning waters.

Charbonneau remained frozen with fear, but Sacajawea, also aboard, did not. She bent over the side of the boat and scooped up most of the fallen cargo back into the pirogue. She did this at great risk to her own life and that of little Jean Baptiste, who was strapped to her back. It was a courageous, selfless act that impressed everyone. If Lewis had any lingering doubts about bringing along the Bird Woman, they were gone now. As for Clark, he took a special interest in Sacajawea and her child — an interest that would outlive the expedition.

On June 2, the company came to a place where the Missouri River played a devious trick on them. The waters branched off in two directions. The explorers had to decide which fork was the true Missouri that would take them westward towards the Pacific. Lewis noted in his journal that taking the wrong fork "would not only lose us the rest of the season but would probably so dishearten the party that it might defeat the expedition altogether."

The two captains, unable to decide which fork was the true one, decided to explore each separately. Two canoes of three men each were sent out to explore each fork. They returned in a short time, still unsure which fork was the Missouri. Lewis and Clark decided to join the searching parties. Clark and one group took the South Fork; Lewis and another group took the North Fork. Clark was quickly convinced he had found the real Missouri.

Lewis, meanwhile, was facing serious trouble on the North Fork. The rafts they had built for the journey had proven unseaworthy and the small party took to the land. Heavy rains had made the shore of the river slippery and treacherous. Lewis slipped from a 90-foot cliff and narrowly saved himself by plunging his spontoon into the earth to stop his fall. No sooner had he gotten back on his feet then, as he later wrote, " . . . I heard a voice behind me cry out, 'God! God! Captain! What shall I do?' On turning, I found it was [Private Richard] Windsor, who had slipped and fallen about the center of this narrow pass and was lying prostrate while he was holding on with the left arm and foot as well as he could . . . I expected, every instant, to see him lose his strength and slip off." Lewis remained calm and instructed Windsor to dig a footing for himself with his knife and crawl to safety. Lewis could only watch helplessly, praying Windsor would have the strength to hold on. Finally, taking his captain's advice, the young man did manage to save himself.

By now, Lewis was convinced this fork was not the Missouri. The other men with him were just as convinced that it was. However, none of them dared to speak up against their leader. To further make his point that the waterway was only a tributary, Lewis named it Maria's River, in honor of his cousin Maria Wood, whom he apparently had a crush on. This was not the first time the captains had renamed a river after a loved one. Shortly before, Clark had persuaded Lewis to rename another tributary, the Bighorn, Judith's River, after a girl he fancied back in Virginia. Clark later learned, to his embarassment, her name was not Judith, but Julia. This didn't stop the lady in question from marrying the explorer soon after his return.

Anxious to prove his North Fork was not the Missouri, Lewis rushed back to the main camp, where Clark was waiting. Four of the party agreed to accompany Lewis on a further trip down the South Fork, from which Clark had just returned. The Mandans had told the explorers that they would come to a series of great waterfalls on the Missouri. Lewis knew if he could find these falls, he was on the right river. The determined captain pressed on, despite the fact that he was suffering from dysentery and a high fever. He treated his illnesses with a remedy of herbal tea and quickly recovered.

On June 13, the small party heard the distant but distinct sound of rushing water. "My ears were saluted with the agreeable sound of a fall of water," observed Lewis, "and, advancing a little further, I saw the spray arise above the plain like a column of smoke . . . I hurried down the hill, to gaze on this sublimely grand spectacle . . . the grandest sight I ever beheld . . . ."

They now knew which way their route lay. As magnificent as the 80-foot high falls were, they presented the explorers with their greatest obstacle yet. The falls would be impossible to go over in the boats. They would have to go around them. This meant building wagons to carry their belongings and canoes a distance of about eighteen miles along steep, difficult terrain. This would eventually bring them back to the river and into Shoshone Indian country where Sacajawea would keep an unexpected appointment with destiny.

7

Strange Homecoming

THIS LEG OF their journey was a great trial for the Corps of Discovery. The men struggled and sweated every inch of the way, hauling their possessions in crude wagons made of cottonwood, the only material at hand. The intense summer heat made the work unbearable. Rainstorms washed out the already uneven trail. Wheels broke and the explorers had to stop to make new ones. Giant mosquitoes bit them mercilessly. It took them two weeks to complete the 18-mile obstacle course around the falls. It was two weeks they would never forget.

The grueling trek put to rest one of the great myths of western exploration — the existence of an easy, direct waterway across the North American continent. Lewis and Clark could now tell President Jefferson with certainty that no such "Northwest Passage" existed.

Once back on the Missouri, Lewis decided to launch an unusual, iron-framed boat he brought along on the expedition. Christened the *Experiment*, the 36-foot vessel was to replace a pirogue they had hidden back at the falls for their return trip. Although the *Experiment* floated "like a perfect cork" at first, according to Lewis, the tar on its bottom cracked and peeled in the hot July sun and the boat quickly sank to the river bottom.

In any case, the *Experiment* would not have been of use to the explorers for very long. The Missouri was rapidly shrinking from a mighty waterway to a twisting mountain stream — shallow and filled with huge boulders and beaver dams. After many miles of traveling by water, the men now faced the prospect of continuing their journey on land. For this they needed horses, not more boats.

Then, as they trudged on, preparing for the work ahead, the Corps of Discovery caught its first glimpse of the Rocky Mountains. They stared in silent awe at the majestic, snow-capped peaks. The mountains' grandeur caused the captains to be both exhilarated and apprehensive. They knew they could never carry their remaining supplies across the towering Rockies without horses, which could only be gotten in trade with the Indians for the remaining gifts and trinkets. But not a single Indian had been seen for months. Were the natives simply afraid, wondered the explorers, or unfriendly? Only time would tell.

On July 22, Clark noticed Sacajawea acting strangely. She began pointing at the countryside and talking rapidly in her native tongue. Charbonneau explained that this was the very spot where she had been kidnapped by the Minnetarees many years before. More importantly, this was the country of her people, the Shoshones. Lewis and Clark took heart at hearing this. Surely the Shoshones would be friendly towards them when they saw that one of their tribe was a member of their party.

Anxious to meet up with the Shoshones, Lewis decided to go ahead of the main party with Drouillard and two others. For two days they saw no sign of Indians. Finally, Lewis spotted through his telescope a lone brave on horseback. He raised a blanket into the air three times as a sign of friendship. The Indian froze, staring at the strangers. The men approached him slowly, holding up other gifts of beads, trinkets, and a mirror. They called out "Tab-ba-bone," which they thought meant "white men" in Shoshone. But to the Indian the words meant something quite different — stranger or enemy. It was an unfortunate misunderstanding. The brave rode off frightened, to spread word of what he believed were enemy invaders.

Soon after, the men came upon three Indian women walking on the trail. One was a young squaw, and at the sight of the explorers she ran for her life. The two older women were too old to flee and, giving up all hope, bowed their heads, expecting death at the hands of the strangers. But Lewis quickly reassured them his intentions were peaceful. He and his men painted the women's cheeks red, a sign of peace they had learned from Sacajawea. The women were overjoyed and agreed to take the strangers to their village at once.

That evening the white men had a powwow with several Shoshone chiefs and smoked the peace pipe.

61

The Bettmann Archive

Sacajawea showing the way toward the Rockies. Although Lewis and Clark at first did not want to allow a woman on the expedition, they soon came to rely heavily on her as a guide and translator. In time, the "Bird Woman" became a central figure among the corp.

Drouillard explained in sign language that the explorers wanted to buy horses from the Indians. The Shoshones, however, had never seen white men before, and were suspicious of them. They feared the men were allies of their enemies, the Blackfeet, who had driven them into the mountains.

A poor tribe, without guns to defend themselves or to hunt for game, the Shoshones were reduced in the winter to living off of edible roots. To show his good intentions, Lewis sent Drouillard and another man off to shoot some game in the nearby forest. They returned a short time later with an antelope and three deer. The Indians were so hungry they ate the animal meat raw, without taking the time to cook it.

Meanwhile Clark and the rest of the party, which had stayed on the river, were having a difficult time navigating their canoes up the narrow, stony stream that the Missouri had become. They finally disembarked not far from the Shoshone village. As they approached Lewis for their rendezvous, a young Shoshone woman rushed to Sacajawea and threw her arms around her. The two women chattered excitedly in their Indian tongue. Clark was surprised to learn that the woman was a childhood friend of Sacajawea's who had also been taken captive by the Minnetarees. She had managed later to escape from her captors, while Sacajawea remained their prisoner.

The party proceeded into the village and Clark joined his partner in the council lodge for another powwow, led by the head chief, Cameahwait. The captains asked

Sacajawea to join them and serve as their interpreter. The Shoshones did not usually allow women into the council lodge, but reluctantly made an exception this time. The explorers sat down cross-legged in the circle of solemn-faced chiefs. After the peace pipe had been passed around, Cameahwait began to speak. Clark turned to Sacajawea for her translation of the chief's words, but she sat staring at Cameahwait, totally speechless. Before Clark could say something to her, she jumped to her feet, grabbed a nearby blanket, and threw it around the chief! Indians and explorers alike were shocked by this unexplainable behavior. Had the Bird Woman lost her senses? Cameahwait angrily tried to push the woman away from him, but she clung to him, weeping and talking excitedly.

"Cameahwait!" Sacajawea cried. "Do you not recognize your long-lost sister?" The great chief stared in astonishment, finally recognizing the little sister he had long ago given up for dead. He now returned her embrace and the solemn powwow turned into a joyful reunion.

Lewis and Clark couldn't have been happier for Sacajawea — or for themselves. Now they would have no trouble getting all the horses they needed to cross the towering Rockies.

The next day, August 18, Lewis celebrated his 31st birthday with an exploratory hike in the Rockies. Then this extraordinary young man, who had already achieved so much in his brief life and would achieve so much more, wrote these words in his journal: "I had

64

in all human probability, now existed about half the period which I am to remain in this . . . world. I reflected that I had as yet done but little, very little, indeed, to further the happiness of the human race, or to advance the information of the succeeding generation." No greater evidence could be found of the dark side of Meriwether Lewis. Even in the glorious dawn of this new world he had discovered, he could not escape his own moody nature.

The Corps of Discovery had now reached a major turning point in their long journey — the great Continental Divide of North America. All rivers on the eastern side of the Rockies flowed east. Those on the western side, flowed west. One of these rivers was the Columbia and, once over the mountains, the explorers would travel on it to their final destination — the Pacific Ocean, or as it was more poetically known, the Western Sea.

On August 30, the party set off to cross the Rockies with twenty-nine horses, a mule, and an Indian guide whom they named Toby that Cameahwait had provided for them. Their "mountain walk," expected to be a simple hike, was, in fact, a ten-day ordeal that left the party exhausted and near starvation.

But relief, and food, were not far away. Clark, with an advance party of hunters, met a group of friendly Nez Perce Indians on their descent. They ate and rested with the Indians and were soon joined by Lewis and the main party. The Nez Perce had never seen white men before and were extremely friendly to their unexpected guests. The tribe was so impressed by the goodwill and courage of the Corps of Discovery, that they would remain friendly with white settlers long after neighboring tribes had gone on the warpath.

On October 7, well rested and refreshed, the explorers set off again in dugout canoes with two Nez Perce chiefs as guides, Twisted Hair and Tetoharsky. They also brought along forty dogs the Indians had sold them. These dogs were not to be companions for Scammon, but serve as food. Dogmeat was a main part of the Nez Perces' diet. At first, the explorers were repulsed by the idea of eating dogs. But to their surprise they soon became fond of dogmeat, no one more so than Captain Lewis. He later wrote in his journal that he was convinced that the men were at their healthiest when on a diet of dogmeat.

The men would indeed need to be at their best, for the waters they were now entering were as dangerous as any they had experienced on the Missouri.

8

The Surging Sea

AT THE SITE of what is now Lewiston, Idaho, the explorers entered the aptly named Snake River, which was filled with twisting, narrow canyons. On October 24, they came into a section of the river known as the Dalles. Here, the rock walls between the boat-shattering rapids were only 45 yards apart. Seeing no place to carry their canoes around the water, Clark was resigned to abandoning them and carrying the supplies up over the steep cliffs. But feisty Pierre Cruzatte sized up the narrow chasm and announced that he could get the canoes down the rushing waters safely.

While the men watched with bated breath, Cruzatte lashed two canoes together and set off down the rapids. The rest of the Corps watched as he steered his frantic path through the rapids and reached the calm waters below safely, without once losing control of the canoes. Cruzatte spent the rest of the day taking all the canoes downriver. Then he stayed up half the night entertaining the local Indians with his fiddle playing.

Six days after entering the Snake River, at the border of present-day Idaho and Washington, the party started down the Columbia. Day by day, they drew closer to their final destination. All around them now they found signs of the Pacific. The tidal waters rose and fell beneath their canoes. The Indians they saw along the land and floating by in canoes were decidedly different from the inland tribes they had encountered previously. These Indians, for good or bad, had dealt with white men before. This meant they had met and traded with the ships of several countries that anchored regularly at the mouth of the Columbia. One Indian they saw wore a British sailor's jacket; another, a Chinook chief, was dressed in a fine coat of blue and scarlet, complete with a sword. The Indians called out to the explorers in broken English, undoubtedly learned from the sailors with which they had come in contact.

Further downriver, the party came upon Indian villages. The inhabitants showed off their proudest possessions to the white men — brass tea kettles and a British musket. Some of the natives had pierced their noses with sea shells and wore round hats and sailor jackets.

The Columbia, at first a twisting, turning obstacle course of treacherous rapids and narrow gorges, had widened into a majestic carpet of blue. Both banks of the river were lined with forests of enormous trees. Lewis noted in his journal that some trees were 200 feet tall and ten feet thick. To him, this seemed exactly the kind of forest that would thrive so near the world's greatest ocean.

November 7, 1805 began as just another day for the members of the Corps of Discovery. The explorers watched and waited for the final sign that they were at the end of their journey — the ocean itself. Suddenly a deep rumble filled the foggy air and quickly rose to a thunderous roar. The weary, skin-soaked men smiled at one another in eager anticipation. The sound could be only one thing — the ocean's waves breaking against the rocky shoreline. Clark was the first to see the open waters. Just before the last Indian village, the dense fog lifted, like some unearthly curtain. There, as if waiting for the most dramatic moment to make its appearance, was the Pacific Ocean. As the rest of the Corps celebrated, Clark, never a good speller, seized his journal and scribbled these words for posterity: "Ocian in view! O! the joy!"

Despite their momentary elation, the men quickly learned there was nothing joyful about the Pacific Northwest coast in winter. It was as inhospitable a setting as any they encountered on their trip. The sharp, jagged rocks of the coastal land made camping difficult. The wet climate made drying out their soaked clothing impossible. The water was forever surging and made many of their party ill with seasickness. Exactly one month after first seeing the Pacific, Clark gave this revised opinion of it in his journal: "I cant say Pacific, as since I have seen it, it has been the reverse."

Soon the party moved to a level site seven miles inland from the ocean where they would spend the winter. They built a fort and named it Clatsop after a friendly Indian tribe that helped them get settled. Here the men of the Corps of Discovery would rest as best they could before beginning the long trip back to St. Louis. But life at Fort Clatsop would in no way resemble the pleasant days spent at Fort Mandan.

In two months' time, the party experienced only four days without rain. The constant downpour dampened both body and spirit. Blankets and clothing rotted, unable to dry out. Many of the men became sick. The Clatsop Indians only added to the company's troubles. Although friendly, they were unkempt and fond of stealing. The captains had to keep an alert eye on them at all times in order to protect their belongings. This was not entirely the Indians' fault. In past years, they had been ill-treated by the fur traders who visited among them. They probably felt that by stealing from the explorers they were getting back what had already been stolen from the tribe by other white men.

Christmas 1805 was an unhappy holiday for the men of Fort Clatsop. Dinner consisted of some foul-smelling fish, a bit of unsalted elk meat, and roots for dessert. There was no whiskey left to raise their spirits, only a little stale tobacco to smoke. New Year's Eve was no better.

However, the men were determined to weather the winter as best they could. They knew once the snows melted, they would be on their way home. As a constructive project, they collected seawater from the

70

ocean and boiled it in big kettles. When all the water boiled away, the salt remained on the insides of the kettles. This was then scraped into barrels. In less than two months, the men obtained twenty gallons of salt, which they used to preserve meat for the long journey back.

One time, a beached whale was discovered on the shore. The men rushed down to strip it of its blubber and add some variety to their diet. But the Indians had gotten there first and they found the whale stripped clean. They later bartered for blubber and whale oil for fuel with the accommodating Indians.

Finally, on March 23, 1806, the explorers were ready to set off for home. Lewis had hoped to have the opportunity to use his "letter of credit" from Jefferson to get them all on board a ship bound for the East coast. However, they sighted no ships along the shore throughout the long winter. A two-masted ship from Boston, the *Lydia*, had twice sailed up the Columbia while Lewis and Clark were there, but both times the parties had missed seeing each other.

Before leaving, the captains wrote a document claiming the territory known as Oregon for the United States government and posted it in the fort. They also wrote a short account of their journey with a map and a list of the party's members. They made copies of the report and left them around the fort. This way, Lewis reasoned, their achievement would be recognized, even if they should not survive the return journey. After this was done, the men loaded the canoes and set off up the

71

Columbia, saying good-bye to the mighty ocean they had traveled more than half a continent to reach.

Unbelievably, the *Lydia* sailed once more up the river only a few days after the men departed. Thus, the Corps of Discovery barely missed an easy, if long, sea passage around Cape Horn and homeward. At the very least, Lewis missed the chance to send a message by sea to Jefferson, letting him know they were alive and well. As it was, the President and the American people had no word from the explorers for over a year. They had given up almost all hope of ever seeing them alive again. They had quite a surprise in store for them!

9

Lewis without Clark

LEWIS DID NOT see their return trip as merely retracing their outgoing route, but rather as an opportunity to further explore the vast wilderness of the West. While the journey back would be shorter and less difficult than the trek west, it would present the explorers with new and unexpected hardships.

Game was not as plentiful as it had been, and the party had to barter for food with the Indians they encountered. Unfortunately, many tribes were not eager to trade once they learned Lewis and Clark had exhausted their supply of gifts. At one point, Lewis was forced to trade his gold-laced military coat and some precious tobacco for an Indian canoe to replace one lost on the river.

Clark dreamed up a clever trick to persuade some stubborn Indians into giving him food. He tossed a charge of slow-burning gun powder wrapped in a paper casing into an Indian tribe's campfire. The fire exploded with bright colors, and the Indians pleaded with Clark to put a stop to the bad magic. The explorer gestured over the campfire at the exact moment he knew the powder would burn out. The Indians immediately gave Clark all the food he wanted.

But it was a real kind of "magic" that proved most useful to the two captains. They used their pills and medical knowledge to treat sick or injured Indians in exchange for food and horses. They had no lack of patients, sometimes treating as many as fifty Indians in a single day. Using the herbal remedies he had learned from his mother and some of the information taught him by Dr. Benjamin Rush, Lewis was a skillful physician. Clark, while lacking Lewis's scientific mind, had the better bedside manner. Together, they treated every problem from rheumatism and dysentery to broken bones and snakebites. Their success rate was amazingly high.

However grateful the Indians were to the white "medicine men," conflicts continued to arise. One tribe, the Chinooks, like the Clatsops, had more than its share of thieves. They even went so far as to steal Lewis's dog. The explorer was enraged and was prepared to fight a tribe of Indians if necessary to get back his prized pet and companion. The warrior who stole Scammon must have realized this, for he gave back the animal without a word of protest.

This experience, and the long months on the trail, were beginning to have their effect on the moody leader of the Corps of Discovery. When he caught another Indian stealing, Lewis hit and kicked the fellow, something he never would have done earlier in the expedition. An entry in his journal reflects this less tolerant attitude towards the natives: "We ordered the sentinel to keep them out of camp and informed them, by signs, that if they made any further attempts to steal our property, or insulted our men, we should put them to death. Our men seem perfectly well disposed to kill a few of them."

Lewis's disposition improved when the party arrived once more in the land of the Nez Perce. They spent nearly a month among this friendly tribe, waiting for the snows of the Rockies' high passes to melt. Only then could they safely cross the rugged mountains.

On June 10, 1806, their impatience got the better of them and they started out again. Although the snow was eight to ten feet high in some places, Lewis and Clark thought it was packed down hard enough for the horses to go over. When they found to their dismay that the snows made the mountain trail too difficult to follow, the explorers decided to turn back. They stored their possessions and started down again to the Nez Perce villages.

Disaster stalked them every step of the frozen, slippery trail. John Colter nearly drowned when his horse fell into a raging stream. Another man nearly bled to death when cut accidentally. For the second time, the party ran out of food and nearly starved. If they hadn't turned back when they did, it is possible the entire expedition may have perished.

Arriving safely among the Nez Perce again, the two

captains convinced several of the Indians to accompany them as guides for a second attempt on the mountains. By now enough of the snow had melted to allow them to get over the pass, although finding food was still a problem. For several days all they had to eat was bear oil and boiled roots, which Lewis, who was by now used to eating nearly anything, called "an agreeable dish."

By the end of June they were below the snow line and pitched camp besides a hot spring. Their Indian guides had the idea of damming up the spring to create a natural hot tub. The entire company striped off their sweaty clothes and enjoyed the first hot bath they had taken in two years.

While resting from their most recent ordeal, Lewis plotted out the next leg of their journey. Always anxious to explore the unknown, he chose a few men to accompany him overland above the Missouri River and then up Maria's River, in search of a shortcut to the Great Falls of the Missouri. Clark and the rest of the party would continue on the same route they had taken west all the way to Jefferson's River, where they had left behind some canoes. Here, Clark's group would split in two. Ten men, led by Sergeant Ordway, would go downstream with the canoes while Clark proceeded on to the previously unexplored Yellowstone River. The plan was for all three groups to reunite when they reached the Missouri.

On July 3, 1806 the captains bid each other farewell. For the first time in the two-year expedition they would be apart for an extended time. In fact, they would not see each other again for nearly six weeks. When they did meet up again, they would have some hair-raising tales to tell.

The gravest danger lay ahead for Lewis and his party. By month's end, Lewis was disappointed to find that the shortcut he was looking for did not exist. Maria's River did not flow north, as he expected, but westward, into the heart of Blackfoot territory. The Blackfeet were a hostile tribe that the Nez Perce had warned Lewis to watch out for. Here, on the Montana plains, the party had a fateful encounter with a party of Blackfeet.

Although suspicious, Lewis was outwardly friendly to the Indians. He smoked the peace pipe with them and allowed them to share the party's camp for the evening. It was a long, tense night for the explorers. They were alert to every sound and movement in the still darkness. When morning came, the Blackfeet made their move. Several braves seized the guns of Reuben Fields and his brother Joseph. The men chased the Indians and a fight broke out. Reuben drew his knife, and in the struggle stabbed one of the Indians in the heart. The brave died instantly.

At the same time, Lewis and Drouillard were under siege by the other Blackfeet. Unable to get the explorers' guns, the braves attempted to steal their horses. They herded the animals towards a ravine, with Lewis pursuing on foot. He cried out that he'd shoot unless the horses were returned at once. One Indian turned and Lewis fired his pistol. The Indian fell, fired at Lewis from the ground, and narrowly missed him. This was enough for the other Blackfeet. They fled the scene, leaving two of their companions lying dead in the dawn's first light. It was the only one of the many encounters the explorers had with Indians that ended in bloodshed.

Lewis wasted no time getting out of Blackfoot country. That day, he and the men covered over a hundred miles across the most rugged terrain. A short time later, by a happy coincidence, they met up with Ordway's party on the banks of the Missouri. But Lewis's troubles were not over. Having escaped death at the hands of hostile Indians, he would soon be lucky to escape it at the hands of one of his own men.

A few days later, at the mouth of the Yellowstone River, Lewis went elk hunting with Pierre Cruzatte. The two hunters separated in the thick brush. Suddenly Lewis felt a sharp pain in his upper thigh. He had been shot, and immediately suspected his partner had done it. "You have shot me!" he cried out.

When Cruzatte didn't respond, Lewis began to worry. Had the Blackfeet followed them, seeking vengeance? Panicked and in great pain, Lewis dragged himself back to camp, where he collapsed. Later, Cruzatte showed up and flatly denied that he had shot his commander. The truth, Lewis guessed, was that his companion had mistaken him for an elk and fired. Later, he wrote in his journal with great understanding, "I do not believe the fellow did it intentionally but, after finding that he had shot me, was anxious to conceal his knowledge of having done so." The wound, though far from fatal, made life miserable for the explorer. It made it impossible for him to sit down or sleep on his back for weeks.

Meanwhile, Clark, by comparison, had a most uneventful journey. The worst trouble his party faced was when Crow Indians stole their horses and pack animals. They were forced to make dugouts from trees and then float on them down the Yellowstone into the Missouri.

On August 12, the two leaders were reunited. Lewis was lying in a pirogue, unable to stand up because of his wound. Clark assumed command and did what he could to quicken his friend's recovery with herbs and medicine. Only two days later, the expedition arrived back in Mandan country. It was an occasion for rejoicing. With any luck, they would be back in St. Louis before the autumn leaves fell. Their magnificent adventure was nearly at its end.

10

Home the Conquering Heroes

BEING BACK AMONG the Mandans was like coming home to old friends for Lewis and Clark. The captains were anxious to bring some of the Mandan chiefs back to Washington with them to meet the "Great White Father" Jefferson. Only one of them, the outgoing Big White, accepted the invitation. The chief would return East with them, accompanied by his wife Yellow Corn and their son.

While among the Mandans, the expedition lost some of its members. John Colter, that rugged frontiersman, collected his pay and headed back into the wilderness. He had no desire to return to civilization. Neither did Charbonneau, whose interpreting skills were no longer needed. This was a sad occasion for Clark. He had grown fond of Sacajawea and her son, Jean Baptiste, who was now over a year old. He even offered to take the boy to St. Louis and pay for his education. Charbonneau, who generally treated Sacajawea more as his property than his wife, may well have resented Clark's concern for his family. He refused the captain's offer, claiming the boy was too young, and departed, taking Sacajawea and the boy with him.

Today, it is difficult to fully determine the role of Sacajawea in the Corps of Discovery. She is often perceived as a legendary guide, without whose help Lewis and Clark would have never found their way across the continent. Others say there is no basis in fact for this claim. There is even some evidence that she was a rather bad guide. When travelling to the Yellowstone River on their return trip, Clark let Sacajawea choose between two passes on their route. Sacajawea chose the Bozeman Pass, which Clark later complained was an "intolerable . . . muddy wet rout." One thing, however, is certain. There is no question that Sacajawea was a courageous and hard-working member of the Corps of Discovery. For that, she has earned her place alongside history's other heroic explorers.

The expedition moved swiftly now, from Mandan country down the wide Missouri towards St. Louis. On September 3, they met two boats heading upstream. The boatmen gave the party their first news of the outside world. Both Lewis and Clark were shocked to hear of the infamous duel between Vice President Aaron Burr and Secretary of the Treasury Alexander Hamilton, in which Hamilton was killed. This was old news to the boatmen, however, as the event had happened two years before.

The explorers took time out of their journey to pay a visit to the grave of Sergeant Floyd, the one member of the expedition who would not be sharing in the glory of their accomplishment. They also bought a gallon of whiskey, the first they had tasted in over a year.

On September 20 the men cheered heartily upon sighting a group of cows grazing contentedly on the grassy riverbank. Later that same day a group of French and American settlers greeted them with shouts and waving from the shore. Clark wrote that the people were "much astonished" to see them. "They informed us that we were supposed to have been long lost since, and were entirely given out by every person."

Three days later they reached St. Louis. Every resident of the growing frontier town turned out to welcome home the conquering heroes. One eyewitness to this historic occasion compared the explorers to "Robinson Crusoes, dressed entirely in buckskins." The company was wined and dined for days; the most humble of their party treated like visiting royalty.

Amid all the festivities, Lewis found time to dash off a letter to his commander-in-chief, the President. He told Jefferson that they had clearly "discovered the most practical rout which does exist across the continent." Lewis ended his report by praising his partner in discovery. "If, sir," he wrote, "any credit be due for the success of that arduous enterprize in which we have been mutually engaged, he is equally with myself entitled to your consideration and that of our common country."

Jefferson responded with "unspeakable joy" at the explorers' safe and successful return. He immediately planned a gala reception in Washington at the President's House. (It would not be called "The White House" for several more years.) The highlight would be a lavish banquet at which Lewis, Clark, and Big White would be the guests of honor.

The captains paid the members of their company their well-earned salaries along with a bonus land grant of 300 acres to each man. Then Lewis and Clark moved on to the Clark homestead near Louisville. Here Clark stayed on, politely declining the President's invitation in order to attend to more pressing business at home. He confided to Lewis that he was off to woo the Virginia girl after whom he had named a river. Her name was Julia Hancock, and despite Clark's infatuation, she knew him only slightly at the time. Lewis bid his friend good-bye and left for Washington with Big White and his family.

The road to Washington was paved with more parties, invitations, and celebrations. When Lewis finally arrived in the capital, three days after Christmas, it was an event comparable to the triumphant return of an astronaut returning from a trip to the moon in our own time. "Never did a similar event excite more joy throughout the United States," wrote one observer.

The banquet Jefferson had promised was one of the most lavish affairs the young capital had ever seen. Seventeen official toasts were drunk to the young explorer's honor, and a poem by Washington poet Joel Barlow entitled "On the Discoveries of Lewis" was recited. In his overblown verse, Barlow compared Lewis to Columbus and ended by calling for the Columbia River to be renamed the Lewis in his honor. Lewis was embarrassed by this suggestion and, although Barlow brought the matter to the attention of Congress, it was never acted upon.

There were, however, other honors that the leaders of the Corps of Discovery did not decline. Lewis and Clark were each granted 1,600 acres of land, Lewis was appointed the Governor of what was then called the Upper Louisiana Territory, and Clark was named the territory's Superintendent of Indian Affairs. Upper Louisiana extended north to Canada and west to the Rocky Mountains — a massive region. Lewis was greatly honored by the appointment, and particularly pleased that he would be working together with his closest friend.

It seemed as if these two young men, both still in their 30s, were to live charmed lives. They had just returned from one of the greatest adventures of their country's history and were now being rewarded for their skill and bravery. They would be governing the new lands they had explored. But there would be no happy ending for one of them.

One of the toasts made at the Washington banquet stated, "May those who explore the desert never be deserted." The words poked fun at the Great American Desert that Lewis and Clark had proven was not a desert at all. Yet these words held a dark, ironic meaning for Governor Meriwether Lewis. In two short years, he would fall from the height of triumph to the depths of despair.

11

Journey's End

ERIWETHER LEWIS WAS in no hurry to get back to St. Louis and his new post as governor of Upper Louisiana. He was thoroughly enjoying all the attention he was receiving as the "conqueror of the Columbia." Every hostess wanted him for her party. Artist and museum curator Charles Wilson Peale made a wax sculpture of him to exhibit in his new Philadelphia Museum. Lewis was truly the toast of the land.

Besides all this, there was the matter of his and Clark's journals to edit and publish. These were much more than a mere narrative of their journey. They included a natural history of the West, a dictionary of 23 different Indian vocabularies, and maps and sketches of wild animals rendered by Clark. The tentative title of this massive, three-volume work was *Lewis and Clark's tour of the Continent of North America, Performed by Order of the Government of the United States During the Year 1804, 1805, and 1806.*

As he labored on this ambitious project, Lewis became concerned that other members of the expedition might come out with their versions of the journey before his and Clark's. He managed to convince all the other would-be authors in the party to wait, with the exception of Patrick Gass, who had been head carpenter for the Corps of Discovery. Gass refused to listen to Lewis, found a publisher, and had the first account of the expedition in print within a year. An uneducated soldier, Gass was smart enough to hire a professional writer from Virginia to polish up his writing and correct his grammar and spelling. While not very good, Gass's journal was accurate in detail and sold well.

Meanwhile, Lewis had more serious problems to worry about. To keep order in St. Louis in his absence, the government appointed Frederic Bates, a Virginia lawyer, to serve as Lewis's secretary and to run the territorial government until his arrival. A worse choice could not have been made.

Bates was a bureaucrat with no real understanding of the West nor the Indians who inhabited it. He, like other politicians back in Washington, saw the new lands as a fresh field for trade and commerce, and little more. He cared nothing about the wilderness, its creatures and lore. Besides this, Bates held a long-standing grudge against Lewis. Years before, Bates's father had recommended his son as a personal secretary for President Jefferson, but the new executive chose Lewis instead. Now Bates, who desperately wanted to be governor, was not only upstaged by Lewis again but had to serve under him. It was too much for the petty man to bear. At the time, Lewis knew nothing of all this, but he would quickly learn.

The new governor finally arrived in St. Louis on March 8, 1808, a full year after his appointment. The little frontier outpost had changed greatly from the time when Lewis and Clark first set out from it in 1804. The French and Spanish officials were gone, replaced by a mixed population of settlers, land speculators, and opportunists of every kind. Many of them wanted the land the Indians inhabited and didn't care how they got it. Others grew rich selling whiskey to the tribes, who quickly developed a self-destructive weakness for the white man's "firewater."

Thirty-three-year-old Governor Lewis was determined to keep peace between the Indians and the new white arrivals. It was a difficult balancing act that required the skills of an adept politician. Lewis was a strong leader but had little stomach for political maneuvering. In temperament, he was ill-suited to be an administrator of government policy, policies with which he often disagreed. Frustrated by the red tape of government bureaucracy, pestered by political enemies jealous of his close relationship with Jefferson, and unable to trust his treacherous assistant, Lewis was soon swamped in his new position.

Then there was the matter of Chief Big White. Lewis had promised Jefferson he would see Big White returned safely to the Mandans. The first escort party sent on this mission was attacked by hostile Indians. Several men were killed and the rest were forced to return

Meriwether Lewis, the daring but moody co-leader of the Corps of Discovery. His triumphant return at the end of the expedition soon turned cold as a result of politics and rivalry. Could the former hero actually have become the victim of a brutal murder?

to St. Louis. A second expedition was successful in getting the chief home, but the cost of the escort parties was questioned by the War Department.

The new Secretary of War, William Eustis, refused to pay several bills, particularly $500 that Lewis used to buy gifts to give to the Indians along the way as protection from attack. Eustis was as insensitive a bureaucrat as Bates. He wrote Lewis a stinging letter that said he could expect no help in his troubles from Jefferson, who had recently left the Presidency after serving two terms. Lewis felt his honor was being questioned and resolved to go to Washington personally to put his case before the new president, James Madison. Bates was delighted by this turn of events and fully expected Lewis to be removed from the governorship, with himself appointed as Lewis's replacement.

On September 4, 1809 Lewis set out from St. Louis for Washington. He planned to travel down the Mississippi to New Orleans, but along the way had second thoughts. British ships were threatening the Gulf of Mexico in a conflict that would erupt later into the War of 1812. Lewis feared he might be captured by the British along with the papers he was carrying. These documents included not only financial records for his defense but also the thirteen hand-written volumes of his and Clark's precious journals. So Lewis changed his route and headed overland to Chickasaw Bluffs, now the city of Memphis, Tennessee. Exhausted both physically and mentally, he stopped at the local military post, Fort Pickering, and stayed there two weeks under the care of the commander, Captain Gilbert Russell. His condition improved, and Russell loaned him $100 to help complete his journey.

On September 29, Lewis resumed his travels, accompanied by Major James Neely, an Indian agent to the Chickasaw tribe. Little is known of Neely, but he appears to have been a somewhat shady character, who encouraged his traveling companion to drink with him. Lewis had previously sworn off hard liquor at the fort, realizing it was bad for his already depressed state of mind. The two men were accompanied by Lewis's Creole servant Pernia and Neely's black servant, who was probably a slave.

By October 6, the travelers arrived at the Natchez Trace, a well-worn Indian trail that extended from Natchez, Mississippi to Nashville, Tennessee. From Nashville, Lewis intended to continue north to Washington. The Trace in those days was a dangerous place, not because of the Indians who lived near it but the white bandits and cutthroats who roamed it. Keel boat men, heading north after selling their boats and goods in New Orleans, often fell prey to these robbers who would kill them, take their money, and bury their bodies in the wilderness.

On the night of October 9, two of Lewis's pack horses escaped from camp. Neely remained behind to find the horses while Lewis, anxious to be on his way, continued on with the servants. He told Neely he would wait for him at the first "white habitation" they came to.

After riding all day, Lewis spotted smoke rising from

a chimney between the trees. He came upon a rough clearing where two crude log cabins stood. This was Grinder's Stand, named after the backwoods couple who ran it as a rustic inn for travelers. Lewis planned to spend the night and be on his way in the morning. He would never leave Grinder's Stand alive.

Mrs. Grinder, whose husband was away at their farm some miles from the cabins, greeted Lewis at the door and agreed to put him up for the night. The servants were to bed down in the stable out in back. Lewis was given the larger cabin and Mrs. Grinder took the smaller one, which also served as a kitchen. Several of her children were with her.

She later told authorities that Lewis seemed nervous and tense. From the other cabin she heard him pacing the floor, talking to himself "like a lawyer." He seemed worried and ate little of the meal she prepared for him. After dinner, he seemed more relaxed and sat in the open doorway smoking a pipe and gazing out at the night. He remarked to his hostess what a "sweet and pleasant night" it was. Then Mrs. Grinder retired to her cabin, and Lewis made his bed on the hard floor with some bear skins and his buffalo robe.

Sometime in the middle of the night, Mrs. Grinder was awakened, according to her testimony, by one or two gunshots. She heard a thud, then groaning and a man's cry for water. Through the chinks in the log wall she saw Lewis stagger around the cabin. She claimed to have been too frightened to open the door and go to his aid, despite his pleas for help. After a while, still calling for water, the badly wounded Lewis stumbled outside into the clearing. Finding no water there, he returned to the cabin and collapsed.

At the first light of dawn, Mrs. Grinder seems to have overcome her fear. She sent one of her children out to the stable to rouse the servants. Pernia and Neely's man rushed in to find Lewis lying on the bed, bleeding from gunshot wounds to the head and side. Lewis, still conscious, begged for Pernia to finish him off, even offering him money to do so. "I'm no coward, but I am so strong," he supposedly whispered. "It is so hard to die." His agony finally ended a few hours later. Neely arrived later that morning and a coroner's jury was hastily gathered the following day. They ruled Lewis's death a suicide.

Did Meriwether Lewis, one of the greatest Americans of his day, die by his own hand? At the time, most Americans believed so, including Thomas Jefferson and William Clark. When news of his friend's death first reached Clark he reportedly exclaimed, "I fear, O! I fear the weight of his mind has overcome him." Today, however, most historians believe that the governor of Upper Louisiana was murdered in cold blood.

The suicide theory has many holes in it. Certainly Lewis was a distressed man on his last journey. He was also ill with fever and prey to the black depression which had always haunted him. Yet there is no evidence that he was drinking heavily at Grinder's Stand. He may well have been rehearsing his prepared speech to the President when Mrs. Grinder heard him talking "like a lawyer." As for talking to himself, such a practice was common among men who spent time alone in the wilderness and was not necessarily a sign of a deranged mind.

As for the charges against him in Washington, while damaging, they were hardly serious enough to drive a man to suicide. Many honorable men of the time were accused of mismanaging money by the penny-pinching bureaucrats in the capital. They survived such charges with their reputations intact. There is no reason to doubt Lewis would have done so as well.

At 35, Meriwether Lewis had everything to live for. The fact that he brought his journals of his famous expedition with him shows he fully intended to complete the trip and get his literary work finally in print. Even if, in spite of all this, we accept the suicide theory, it is difficult to understand how such an expert marksman and courageous individual could have so badly botched the job as to cause himself such suffering.

If Lewis was murdered, who killed him and why? One motive is clear and simple — robbery. Lewis was carrying $200 on him, including the money Russell had lent him; quite a considerable sum in those days. Travelers along the Natchez Trace had their throats cut for far less. Identifying the murderer at this point is more difficult, if not impossible. We may never know for certain what took place in the early hours of October 11, 1809 in that crude, Tennessee cabin. That doesn't mean we can't have theories.

The most likely suspect is the mysterious Robert

Grinder. Did he return to the cabins that night and, with his wife's assistance, rob and murder their guest? Mrs. Grinder's story has never quite made sense. Why should a toughened frontier woman, handy with a rifle, be so deathly afraid of going to the aid of a man she knew was gravely wounded and could do her little harm? As for her husband, he must have been a disreputable character. Many neighbors in the area, including supposedly the members of the coroner's jury, suspected him of murdering Lewis, although there was no evidence to prove the accusation against him or anyone else.

Then there is Pernia, Lewis's mysterious servant. Lewis owed him a large sum of money in back wages. Did Pernia kill his master to get the money? The servant disappeared a short time after and was reported to have died as a suicide about a year later. Did he kill himself out of guilt for murdering Meriwether Lewis?

And what about the absent Major Neely? Did he have a hand in his traveling companion's death? He kept Lewis's pistols, never returning them to the dead man's family, and may have stolen other of Lewis's possessions as well. Could such a man also be capable of murder?

These are the known suspects. Some historians are convinced his killer was simply one of the notorious land pirates along the Trace. They easily could have trailed Lewis to the cabin and then made their attack under cover of darkness. If this is what happened,

Lewis put up a brave and valiant fight that drove off his assailant or assailants before they finished the deed.

Lewis was buried in a careless grave a short walk from the cabin where he met his untimely end. For years, the grave was as neglected and forgotten as the memory of the great explorer himself. The shame of suicide cast a stain on Lewis's reputation that only in relatively recent years has been removed. In later life, William Clark reversed his opinion and was convinced his old friend was murdered. History seems to have agreed with him.

Clark's later years tell a far happier story. In 1812, Congress organized the Missouri Territory, which included St. Louis and a sizable piece of Upper Louisiana. Clark, who had turned down the governorship once before, accepted when offered it again. Frederic Bates, who so resented Meriwether Lewis, served under Governor Clark for seven years. Ironically, the two men got along well enough and Clark had no trouble from his subordinate.

Perhaps the greatest contribution Clark made in his later years, was as Superintendent of Indian Affairs. Like his late friend, he had a deep sympathy for the Indians, matched by few other white Americans in the 1800s. He worked hard to keep whites from illegally settling on tribal lands, and tried to keep dishonest traders from selling whiskey to the Indians. Clark meted out justice fairly to both Indians and whites who broke the law. He even created a museum to display Indian artifacts and "curiosities." The Indians, in turn, treated him with great respect and affection, calling him "Red Head Chief."

In 1820, Clark's beloved wife Julia died. After a period of deep mourning, he married her first cousin, Harriet Kennerly, who had grown up with Julia. Clark had met them both for the first time on the same day many years before. William and Harriet had two children, adding to the three surviving children from his first marriage.

The oldest of his children was Meriwether Lewis Clark, named after his great friend. Meriwether Clark was a credit to his namesake. He served bravely in the Black Hawk Indian War of the early 1830s and later fought on the side of the Confederacy as an officer in the Civil War.

Harriet died in 1831 and William survived her by seven years. He died at his son's home on September 1, 1838, one month after his sixty-eighth birthday. He was buried in St. Louis, the city that had played so important a part in his long career as an explorer and administrator. Clark's funeral procession, it was reported, was a mile long.

That is the story of Lewis and Clark. But what about the other brave members of their famous expedition? Their lives after that great adventure were as varied and different as that of their two leaders. Some, like John Colter, returned to the wilderness where they felt most at home. Colter, after exploring what is today Yellowstone National Park, retired from fur trapping and settled down on a farm in La Charrette, home of Daniel Boone. He married an Indian woman, and died in 1813.

York was given his freedom by Clark, who helped set him up in the freight-handling business. The former slave died of cholera soon after in Tennessee.

George Shannon, the youngest member of the party, no sooner got back from the Pacific, than he turned around for another trip up the Missouri with some other members of the Corps of Discovery. This time, fortune was not with him. They ran into a party of Sioux who attacked them savagely. Four men died and nine were wounded, including Shannon. His leg was so badly hurt that it had to be amputated. This didn't stop the energetic young man from making a name for himself in the world. He went on to become a lawyer and state senator from the new state of Missouri. He died in 1838.

Patrick Gass, that defiant Irishman, fought in the War of 1812 and lost an eye in combat. He married at age sixty and had seven children. He lived to the ripe old age of 98, dying in 1870. Nathaniel Pryor also fought in the War of 1812 and later became an Indian trader. He married an Indian and died among her tribe, the Osages, in 1831. John Ordway settled down in Missouri, married and became a well-to-do landowner.

Other expedition members had less happy endings. George Drouillard, whose abilities and character Lewis praised to Jefferson upon their return, went back to the Rocky Mountains. He died tragically at the hands of a band of Blackfoot Indians near Three Forks in 1810, only a year after Lewis's death. Blackfeet warriors also took the lives of John Potts and that merry fiddler, Pierre Cruzatte.

Sacajawea's fate is less certain. Like much of her life, her death is shrouded in legend. It was reported she died of a fever in St. Louis in 1812. However, some historians claim she lived till 1869, when she was killed by a war party from an enemy tribe. Still others say she left Charbonneau and married a Comanche warrior. When he died in battle, she went to live with a band of Shoshones and died at an amazingly old age in 1884.

As for Charbonneau, he lived out his days among the Indians and died in 1840, at the age of 80. Long before, he brought his family to St. Louis and left Jean Baptiste in the care of William Clark. Clark took care of the boy as if he were his own son. He sent him to school and later to Europe, where Sacajawea's son studied philosophy and literature. He returned to the West and became a well-known guide and interpreter for Western travelers. Among the many people he led west was William Clark's son Jefferson. Jean Baptiste died in Oregon 1885 at the age of 80 — the last survivor of the Corps of Discovery.

12

The Legacy of Lewis and Clark

THE IMMEDIATE ACHIEVEMENT of Lewis and Clark's expedition was a stunning one, as apparent to us today as it was to Americans back in 1806. They traveled nearly 7,700 miles with twenty-nine men over mostly unexplored territory filled with dangers of every kind. Over a period of almost two and a half years, they lost only one member of their company under circumstances that probably had nothing to do with the hardships they faced. Their dealings with the many Indian tribes they encountered were mostly friendly, and only once were they forced to resort to bloodshed. They made their incredible journey with only one keel boat, several dugouts and canoes, and a minimum of provisions. Compare their record with any other exploratory expedition before or since, and the leadership abilities of Lewis and Clark are all the more remarkable.

In light of all this, it is interesting to note that one specific goal of their mission ended in failure. Jefferson had hoped the explorers would find a direct trade route across the continent to the Pacific. Clark's painstaking map of their journey from Fort Mandan to Fort Clatsop proved beyond a doubt that no such easy water route existed. The Missouri did not flow comfortably into the Columbia.

However, this disappointment was to be a small one. Much more importantly, the expedition strengthened the United States' claim to the Oregon Territory, rich in furs and fertile farmland. The rain-swept Pacific coast that the explorers couldn't wait to leave, proved a gold mine for the enterprising businessman John Jacob Astor only a few years later. Astor's agents followed Lewis and Clark's trail to the coast in 1811, and established a small fur-trading post near Fort Clatsop at the mouth of the Columbia. They named it Astoria, after their employer, and it became the first permanent American settlement west of the Rockies. The flourishing fur trade at Astoria helped make John Jacob Astor the first millionaire in America.

Many other Americans were inspired by the success of the Corps of Discovery. Lewis and Clark had shown the nation that the land beyond the Mississippi was not a great desert but a wilderness full of natural beauty, wonders, and vast resources. They fired the imagination of Americans tired of life in the crowded cities of the East and opened up a world of opportunity and adventure for these future pioneers. While the rugged path Lewis and Clark took west proved impractical for immigration, they provided the spark that set off a westward movement that would continue for the next sixty years.

The settling of the West was probably inevitable, but without Lewis and Clark it may well have taken a lot longer to get started.

Of nearly equal importance is the contribution the explorers made to our knowledge of the natural history of the West. They were the first white Americans to discover and study 178 plants, 122 animals, and 24 Indian tribes. The animals they sent specimens of included the prairie dog, pronghorn antelope, jackrabbit, pelican, coyote, and porcupine. Two of the birds they discovered bear their names today — "Lewis's woodpecker" and "Clark's crow."

The captains treated the Indians they met with respect and dignity. They studied their languages and noted their customs. They collected examples of their artistry and craftsmanship. Sadly, most of the bonds of friendship they established with the tribes were later to be broken. The traders and settlers who followed Lewis and Clark west did not bring gifts and goodwill. They brought instead disease, dishonesty, and death. A little over thirty years after the explorers spent a happy winter among the Mandans, the tribe was wiped out by an epidemic of small pox, introduced by passing settlers.

The men who followed Clark in managing Indian affairs lacked his understanding and admiration for these native peoples. They saw the Indians as an obstacle and threat to Western expansion. The result was a series of Indian wars that doomed the great Western tribes to a pitiful existence on government-controlled reservations. This was directly opposed to the beliefs of Lewis and Clark. Both men spent their lives trying to see the Indians' rights upheld despite the advancement of white settlements. Their failure to achieve this was not from lack of trying.

The journals the explorers so carefully kept and constantly polished and refined have become a classic of American literature, as well as one of the outstanding records of exploration in modern history. The story that led to its publication is a fascinating one, well worth retelling.

After Lewis's death at Grinder's Stand, Major James Neely, who had retrieved the two pack horses carrying the journals, had the manuscripts sent on to the War Department in Washington. The journals were hardly in a condition to be published. They consisted of hundreds of loose, handwritten pages, unbound and bundled in leather. Seven of the thirteen bundles were written by Lewis, six by Clark.

The journals soon came into William Clark's possession. He made it his top priority to get them published to honor his dead friend's memory. From Virginia, Clark wrote to 24-year-old Nicholas Biddle, a busy Philadelphia lawyer, asking him to take on the formidable task of editing the 1,200,000 words of text. Biddle had graduated from Princeton University at fifteen, then served as secretary to the United States ambassadors to both France and Great Britain. Biddle agreed to serve as editor, while Clark turned over the scientific data from the journals to Dr. Benjamin Barton, another Philadelphian.

Unfortunately, Barton died suddenly before he could work on the manuscript, and this wealth of information remained lost for years to come.

Biddle did a thorough job editing the journals. He not only corrected the spelling and grammar, but organized the narrative into chapters and added his own sophisticated style to the plain prose of the explorers. The work was ready for publication by 1812, but the war with the British that began that year made it difficult to find a publisher. Finally, on February 20, 1814, the journals of Lewis and Clark made their appearance in print with an introductory essay by Thomas Jefferson on the life of his late friend, Meriwether Lewis.

Surprisingly, the journals made little impression at first. Only 2,000 copies were printed and those sold poorly. Over 500 copies mysteriously disappeared, perhaps burned in a fire. The poor sales were partially due to the continuing War of 1812 and partially to the tarnished reputation of Lewis, an apparent suicide. Total profits for the first edition were $154.10, none of which went either to Clark or to Lewis's heirs.

Gradually the work was recognized for the classic adventure tale it is, and it was reprinted many times throughout the nineteenth century. A fuller edition, including one volume devoted exclusively to Clark's maps, was published in 1893. But the editor, Dr. Elliott Coues, added his own florid style and departed further from the simple, direct style of the original authors. About fifteen years later, a special centenary edition in eight volumes edited by R. G. Thwaites was published.

It is considered by scholars to the most complete and accurate edition of the journals of Lewis and Clark.

But the last word on the journals was still to come. In January 1953 an amazing discovery was made in St. Paul, Minnesota. Inside an old, dusty rolltop desk in the attic of a Victorian house were found the original field notes William Clark had written at Wood River, before the official start of the expedition. The notes, in Clark's handwriting, were contained on 67 scraps of paper, some only three inches long.

How did these extraordinary documents get in this desk? The desk belonged to Civil War general John Henry Howard who died in 1890. Howard, who worked for years in the Bureau of Indian Affairs, had known Clark personally as a young man. How he got his hands on the explorer's notes from a previously little-known period remains a mystery to this day.

The federal government claimed the notes as their property because they were part of an official report by Clark, who was a United States Army officer at the time. Historians and museum curators shuddered to think of those precious historical papers being locked away from view by the army. The matter went to a four-day trial which the government lost. Clark's notes were given to Yale University which had them published in 1964.

Interest in the expedition of Lewis and Clark remains as keen today as ever. Perhaps their final legacy lies in the journey itself and what it has come to mean to generations of Americans. The adventure and romance of those unforgettable two and a half years over trails, rivers, and mountains has never lost its appeal. There is a sense of purpose, a spirit of adventure, and a thirst for knowledge embodied by these two men that represents the best our country has to offer. Their spirit, courage, and unfailing friendship is something that is, and will remain, a cherished part of our national heritage.

APPENDIX 1

MEMBERS OF THE CORPS OF DISCOVERY
(1804–1806)

Leaders: Captain Meriwether Lewis and Second Lieutenant William Clark (considered equal in rank during expedition)

Sergeants: Charles Floyd (only member to die on journey), Patrick Gass (promoted from private upon Floyd's death), John Ordway, and Nathaniel Pryor

Privates: William Bratton, John Collins, John Colter, Pierre Cruzatte, Joseph Fields, Reuben Fields, Robert Frazier, George Gibson, Silas Goodrich, Hugh Hall, Thomas Procter Howard, Francis Labiche, Jean Baptiste Lapage (recruited at Fort Mandan), Hugh McNeal, John Potts, George Shannon, John Shields, John B. Thompson, William Werner, Joseph Whitehouse, Alexander Willard, Richard Windsor, and Peter Wiser

Civilians: Toussaint Charbonneau (hired at Fort Mandan), George Drouillard (Drewyer), Sacajawea (Charbonneau's Indian wife), Jean Baptiste (their son born on the expedition,

February 11, 1805), and York (Clark's servant).

Soldiers who traveled only as far as Fort Mandan: Corporal Richard Warfington and Privates John Boley, John Dame, Ebenezer Tuttle, and Isaac White. Privates John Newman and Moses Reed were members of the permanent party, but were court-martialed and sent back to St. Louis.

APPENDIX 2

EXPLORERS OF THE WEST WHO CAME AFTER LEWIS AND CLARK

Lewis and Clark inspired many others to follow in their footsteps. Here are some of the more important people who explored the West after them.

Explorers	Regions Explored	Dates of Exploration
Zebulon Pike— U.S. Army lieutenant	Mid-west, Spanish New Mexico, and Rocky Mountains, but never climbed the mountain that bears his name, Pike's Peak.	1805–1807
John Colter— mountain man, former member of Corps of Discovery	What is now Yellowstone National Park.	1807–1810

James Bridger—mountain man, guide	The Great Salt Lake region of Utah. Blazed Oregon Trail.	1824–1825, 1843
Jedediah Smith—mountain man, trader	The Great Basin region of Utah. Blazed trails to California and Pacific Northwest.	1824–1829
John Charles Fremont—U.S. Army officer. Later became U.S. Senator, and Territorial Governor of Arizona	Much of the far West between the Rockies and the Pacific.	1842–1846

APPENDIX 3

MEMORIALS AND MONUMENTS ALONG THE TRAIL OF LEWIS AND CLARK

The Western trail of Lewis and Clark has largely disappeared in the nearly two hundred years since they traveled it, but there are still reminders of their great adventure that you can visit and see today. Here are a few of them:

Monticello — Thomas Jefferson's home outside Charlottesville, Virginia, is now a museum. It was here that Jefferson planned the great trek west with his young secretary, Meriwether Lewis. This unique mansion, which Jefferson designed himself, is an extraordinary memorial to this great President's vision and imagination.

Jefferson Memorial Museum — This museum, located in the Forest Park section of St. Louis, Missouri, contains historic Western relics and the original documents pertaining to the Louisiana Purchase.

Mandan Lodge — This rebuilt Indian lodge stands on the site of a Mandan village visited by Lewis and Clark near Mandan, North Dakota.

Statue of Sacajawea with her child — This memorial

to the heroic woman of the Corps of Discovery stands in Bismarck, North Dakota.

Fort Clatsop — Lewis and Clark's second winter headquarters has been faithfully reconstructed by the Oregon Historical Society just south of the town of Astoria, Oregon.

Meriwether Lewis National Monument — This park includes the site of Grinder's Stand, where Lewis died in 1809 under mysterious circumstances, the explorer's grave, and a section of the infamous Natchez Trace, the old trail on which Lewis made his final journey.

William Clark's Tomb — This impressive monument to Lewis's partner in discovery is located in St. Louis and is topped by a bust of the explorer.

Other books you might enjoy reading

1. Bakeless, John. *The Adventures of Lewis and Clark.* Houghton Mifflin, 1962.

2. Chidsey, Donald Barr. *Lewis and Clark: The Great Adventure.* Crown, 1970.

3. DeVoto, Bernard. *The Journals of Lewis and Clark.* American Heritage, 1963.

4. McGrath, Patrick. *The Lewis and Clark Expedition.* Silver Burdett, 1985.

5. Viola, Herman J. *Exploring the West.* Smithsonian Books, 1987.

About the Author

Steven Otfinoski is the author of many young adult novels and nonfiction books, including *Mikhail Gorbachev: The Soviet Innovator* and *Jesse Jackson: A Voice for Change* in the Great Lives series. His own biography recently appeared in the prestigious reference book on young adult writers, *Something About the Author*.

Mr. Otfinoski is also a professional playwright with numerous productions in New York City and regional theater. His most recent play, "Still Life with Dead Grizzly," is about the life and mysterious death of explorer Meriwether Lewis. He lives in Stratford, Connecticut, with his wife and two children.